BRANDED
for IMPACT

UNLEASHING YOUR PERSONAL BRAND

Stacey Ruth

Stacey Ruth
CEO/Founder
The Unstoppable Leader
www.unstoppable-leader.com

Book Layout ©2013 BookDesignTemplates.com

Ordering Information:
Quantity sales. Special discounts are available on quantity purchases by corporations, associations, and others. For details, contact the "Special Sales Department" at Unstoppable-Leader.com.

Branded for Impact: Unleashing Your Personal Brand / Stacey Ruth. —1st ed.
ISBN 979-8-8638922-0-7

Contents

This book is the result of countless people encouraging and believing in my voice and my vision. Most of all though, it is the result of my husband, Barron, reminding me to stay true to my own brand, and remain unstoppable.

*Don't be scared to present the real you to the world,
authenticity is at the heart of success.*

—ANONYMOUS

CHAPTER 1

The Power of Your Brand

Because you chose this book, you are probably looking for a stronger personal brand. By the same token, you also are not entirely confident you know how to cultivate it, or where to begin. So, at the risk of repeating a few things you may already have a clue about, let's get very clear about what a personal brand can do for you, and also what it cannot.

Personal branding refers to the process of creating a *unique and authentic* image and reputation for oneself. It involves consciously shaping and managing how others perceive and associate with you. In today's hyper-connected and competitive world, personal branding has become increasingly significant and powerful. Yet it continues to be under-utilized and widely misunderstood.

If you want to differentiate yourself in order to advance your career or your business, you will be hard pressed to do so without establishing an *intentional* personal brand. Your personal brand is the one thing that can ensure you stand out from the crowd. It helps you establish a distinct identity and showcase your unique qualities, skills, and expertise. By highlighting what sets you apart, you can position yourself as a specialist or thought leader in your field, making it easier for others to remember and recognize you.

Whether you are climbing the career ladder or starting and building a business, a strong personal brand can significantly impact your career progression. It enhances your visibility and credibility, making it more likely for you to be considered for new opportunities, promotions, partnerships, or collaborations. In fact, a well-crafted personal brand can attract attention from employers, clients, and influencers, opening doors to exciting prospects.

To be clear, however, being *intentional* about your brand, and *crafting* it for greater visibility and impact does not equate to being inauthentic or outright fake. We each have strengths worth showcasing. And, by the same stroke, we have weaknesses we would prefer to minimize or eliminate. A successful, intentional personal brand puts the spotlight on what's working, and is careful to not misrepresent skills, talents or expertise that are still "under construction."

Think about it this way – if a consumer brand promised great price and value, but then, when you got to the point of purchase, the add-ons and upselling you were asked to accept for even the most basic options were many times over that initial price, you would feel tricked and lied to. And that is precisely what we want you to avoid doing in your own brand *at all costs.*

Your authentic brand is what will create the influence you need to advance yourself and grow. Its authenticity builds trust and fosters positive relationships. When you consistently demonstrate your expertise as it actually is, people are more likely to view you as a reliable source of information or a trusted advisor. This trust can translate into increased influence and the ability to inspire and motivate others, whether within your industry, your community, or on a broader scale.

Personal branding also facilitates networking and relationship-building. As you cultivate a strong personal brand, you attract like-minded you who resonate with your values and interests. These connections can lead to valuable collaborations, mentorship opportunities, and mutually beneficial partnerships. Networking becomes easier when people recognize and understand what you bring to the table. So it is critical to understand that if you are inauthentic in any way, you are likely to attract the wrong people and opportunities!

Your true brand will provide you with a competitive edge and greater adaptability in a rapidly evolving job market. You don't need to dress it up as something else other than what it is. By building a reputation based on your real skills, knowledge, and adaptability, you become more resilient to changes in your industry or the economy. Your personal brand becomes a portable asset that can be leveraged in different contexts and can support career transitions or entrepreneurial endeavors.

Ultimately, engaging in cultivating your personal brand is not just about how others perceive you; it also involves self-reflection and self-improvement. Your brand is about you, and when you engage is developing your brand, you are engaging in self-development.

To build an authentic personal brand, you need to understand your strengths, values, and passions. This introspection can lead to personal growth, increased self-awareness, and a clearer sense of purpose, which can positively impact all aspects of your life.

It's essential for all these reasons to begin based on authenticity, integrity, and consistency. Instead of worrying about creating a false or exaggerated image, focus instead on showcasing the best version of yourself and aligning your actions with your personal brand. With the power of personal branding, you can shape your own narratives, create opportunities, and leave a lasting impact in your chosen fields.

The Importance of Branding in Today's World

Personal branding plays a crucial role in creating your own adaptability in a dynamic world by enabling you to respond to changing circumstances, industry trends, and market demands. While this might seem like a stretch for what a personal brand is capable of, especially if you just want to grow your visibility and maybe grab that career promotion for yourself, it is a very powerful aspect that ought not be dismissed too quickly. When you decide to tap into personal branding you get all its power, not just select bits and pieces. So, look out!

With self-awareness comes awareness of your surroundings, including industry and market shifts. Developing a personal brand requires you to stay attuned to industry trends and changes in the market. This is a non-negotiable for lasting brand building. It involves continuous learning, research, and monitoring of relevant developments.

By actively engaging with the industry and staying informed, you can identify emerging opportunities and potential disruptions. You will likely also become a thought leader, regardless of whether that was on your radar, or not. This awareness allows you to adapt your personal brand accordingly, and with relative speed, aligning your skills, expertise, and messaging with the evolving needs of the market.

In today's world, you may have noticed, market needs and expectations shift rapidly. Personal branding, done intentionally, with ongoing awareness and cultivation, provides the flexibility to adjust positioning and messaging to align with new market demands. You can showcase your ability to adapt, highlight relevant experiences or projects, and emphasize transferable skills that resonate with evolving industry requirements.

You may evolve and adapt, but your personal brand, at its core, is constant. From that core of constancy, you can evolve and alter the focus on certain individual qualities as appropriate. When you are crystal clear about who you are, growth becomes inevitable.

The digital age has brought about significant changes in how we communicate and engage with others. It is an essential skill to understand how to leverage digital platforms and technologies to reach a wider audience, establish an online presence, and showcase expertise. By embracing new technologies, you become able to adapt to changing communication channels and engage with your target audience effectively. Additionally, when you stay updated on emerging platforms, such as social media networks or industry-specific platforms, and leverage them to connect with others, and share your unique insights, it is unavoidable that you will build your brand in the process.

Your ability to pivot personally and professionally has never been more necessary than it is today. If you haven't experienced it for yourself yet, you are probably aware the time is coming for you to make strategic shifts, such as changing careers, pursuing new ventures, or exploring different industries.

Ultimately, your brand is far more than a narrative, a voice, and a mission. It fosters your ongoing personal evolution.

What Your Personal Brand Cannot Fix

At this point you might think strengthening your personal brand is a cure-all for every professional challenge, from career advancement to client acquisition. Unfortunately, although it can be a powerful tool for building a positive reputation and influencing how others perceive you, there are certain things it cannot fix.

Lack of Competence: Personal branding alone cannot compensate for a lack of skills, knowledge, or expertise in a particular field. Many clever online gurus are suckering the eager business start-ups with false claims and outright lies. While branding can create an initial positive impression, it is essential to back it up with substance and deliver on your promises.

Ethical Issues: If someone has engaged in unethical behavior or has a history of questionable actions, personal branding cannot completely repair the damage caused. Genuine personal growth and a commitment to ethical conduct are necessary to rebuild trust and credibility.

Poor Product or Service Quality: If the products or services you offer are subpar, personal branding alone cannot make up for the deficiencies. Ultimately, customer satisfaction relies on the value and quality provided, and no amount of branding can compensate for a disappointing product.

Negative Reputation: While personal branding can help shape a new narrative and improve your image, it may not entirely erase a negative reputation or past mistakes. Changing perceptions takes time, consistent actions, and a genuine commitment to personal growth.

Lack of Alignment with Values: If your personal brand does not align with your true values, beliefs, or passions, it can create inconsistency and dissonance. Building a strong personal brand requires authenticity and being true to oneself rather than merely adopting an image that is disconnected from your core identity.

External Circumstances: Personal branding may not be enough to overcome external factors beyond your control, such as economic downturns, industry shifts, or market conditions. While personal branding can enhance your visibility and opportunities, it does not guarantee immunity from external challenges.

Personal branding is a means to express and communicate your authentic self and value proposition. It can amplify your strengths, create opportunities, and enhance your influence, but it cannot solve underlying issues or compensate for fundamental shortcomings.

The Daunting Side of Personal Branding

Let's assume you have great skills and expertise, and there are no skeletons in your closet. You still might harbor a few doubts about how "all in" you want to go on this personal brand development, especially if it means you might be undergoing a rebranding or reinvention as a part of the process.

Although reinventing one's personal brand can be an exciting prospect, it is also natural to experience fear or hesitation.

There is a quality of the unknown in any creative process. That is why it takes courage. Stepping into the unknown can be intimidating to the most accomplished achievers among us. Reinventing a personal brand means venturing into new territory, which can bring uncertainty about the outcomes or the reception of the changes. Fear of failure or making mistakes can hold a lot of highly qualified folks back from taking the leap.

It also is true that changing one's personal brand may invite judgment or criticism from others. You may worry about how your family, friends, colleagues, clients, or society at large will perceive a reinvention. After all, they like and love you the way you are now. Why risk that? If that resonates for you, it is important to remember that fear of negative opinions or rejection has deterred many, otherwise bold, entrepreneurs and executives from embracing change. You are not alone. But that fear also keeps us stuck where we are right now. Upleveling means fresh visibility, which means fresh vulnerability. Yet it is the only way forward.

Personal brands are often closely tied to an individual's identity and sense of self. Reinventing one's brand can mean letting go of familiar aspects of identity, which can be unsettling. Fear of losing one's identity or not being recognized for who they have been for long periods of time can create resistance to change.

Although rebranding or brand-building can sound exciting initially, the effort itself takes time and energy. Reinvention may require you to start from scratch, reestablish your reputation, or rebuild your networks. If you are starting to build or rebuild your brand after allowing yourself to become burnt out, or during a crisis of finances or career threats, when you don't feel you have the luxury of time, you might be tempted to throw in the towel.

Additionally, many high-achievers—especially those who find themselves in a role where they are first, only, or different—may have an added challenge of battling imposter syndrome. This is one of the biggest challenges entrepreneurs deal with today at every stage of business, and it refers to the feeling of inadequacy, and the fear of being exposed as a fraud despite evidence of competence. It makes a balanced self-assessment almost impossible until the syndrome is addressed. Regardless, when considering a personal brand reinvention, you may question your skills, qualifications, or ability to live up to the new image they want to project.

Even if imposter syndrome is not at issue, reinventing your personal brand may disrupt your current stability or security—at least temporarily. Even a disappointing or underwhelming situation in the present moment can give you a sense of security. Why risk that during a transition where the results are uncertain, and the timeframe is unclear. You might worry about potential financial repercussions or the impact on personal and professional relationships. Modifying your personal brand in any way is inherently a risk—as is remaining exactly where you are. But it is a risk nonetheless.

Even with all these reasons to turn back from revising your personal brand, by far the people with the greatest fear about enhancing or recreating your personal brand are those who have achieved success based on their current personal brand.

If it ain't broke, why fix it?

This may be true, but consider the rate that technology is advancing. Tech that is more than five years old simply cannot perform the functions you need it to do. That's true of your brand as well. What worked then becomes less and less functional over time. Fear of letting go of past accomplishments or the belief that the current brand defines your worthiness can create resistance to the very change that is necessary in order to keep you thriving.

Overcoming these fears requires self-reflection, courage, and a willingness to embrace growth. Seeking support from mentors, friends, or professionals can provide guidance and reassurance during the reinvention process. It is important to remember that fear is a normal part of change, and with proper planning and determination, you can successfully navigate the challenges and reap the rewards of a reinvented personal brand.

When to Avoid Rebranding Yourself

While rebranding (or simply branding) yourself is usually a great thing – it's not always the right answer. We can often dwell on the fears listed above, and miss the real dangers of reinvention and rebranding in the process. Here are a few scenarios where creating a new personal brand for yourself could be a potentially negative, or problematic, choice:

Lack of Genuine Motivation:

If someone seeks to reinvent themselves solely to please others or conform to societal expectations without genuine personal motivation, it can lead to a loss of authenticity and a disconnection from one's true self. It's important to ensure that the desire for reinvention stems from personal growth and fulfillment rather than external pressures.

Extreme and Disruptive Changes:

Radical or impulsive reinventions without careful thought and planning can be disruptive and destabilizing. It's crucial to consider the potential impact on personal relationships, financial stability, and overall well-being. Drastic changes that are not well-considered or aligned with one's values and goals can lead to unintended negative consequences.

Ignoring Personal Development and Healing:

Sometimes, you may use reinvention as an escape or avoidance strategy to evade personal issues or unresolved trauma. It's essential to address underlying emotional or psychological challenges and prioritize personal growth and healing before embarking on a reinvention journey. Failing to do so can perpetuate underlying issues and hinder long-term well-being.

Impersonating or Manipulating Others:

Reinventing yourself should never involve intentionally deceiving or manipulating others. It's crucial to maintain ethical standards and integrity throughout the process. Any attempt to misrepresent oneself or exploit others for personal gain is unethical and can have damaging consequences.

Disregarding Your Own Core Values and Beliefs:

While reinvention allows for growth and change, it's important to ensure that the process remains true to one's core values and beliefs. If the reinvention leads to a significant misalignment with one's authentic self, it can result in a loss of identity and personal fulfillment.

Neglecting Self-Acceptance:

Reinvention should not be driven by a desire to escape or reject aspects of oneself that are deemed undesirable or flawed. Self-acceptance is an essential part of personal growth, and genuine reinvention should involve embracing and integrating all aspects of oneself rather than trying to reject or suppress them.

It is crucial to approach your personal branding journey with self-reflection, self-awareness, and a genuine desire for personal and professional growth. It is an extremely powerful tool for growing your influence and impact in the world. To engage in this work is to tap your own inner, essential power, which many of us have kept hidden from ourselves and the world without even knowing it. This book is designed to bring your authentic strengths, skills and ability to serve the world out into the light where it belongs. It's time your personal brand was unleashed.

CHAPTER 2

A Brand New You

No one can be you, except you. And you cannot be anyone else. That is the essence of a personal brand. You are this amazing, miraculous work in progress—ever-evolving, fascinatingly one-of-a-kind, and totally worth knowing. You don't stand still. You have things to do in your life! You have a goal and a vision for where you are headed. And your brand can lead the way, evolving with you.

Your personal brand encompasses all the unique qualities, values, skills, experiences, and perceptions that distinguish you. It is the DNA of who you are in this moment. Capturing that DNA, distilling it into a clear, coherent voice and visual presence, both online and offline, defines how you are perceived by others. Owning your personal brand means owning your reputation and image.

To do this thoroughly and effectively involves cultivating a strong and memorable personal narrative, maintaining a positive online presence, and actively managing one's reputation. This translates into actively defining your target audience, understanding your needs and aspirations, and aligning your skills and expertise to provide value for them, most especially. It requires consistent and authentic self-expression through various channels, such as social media, personal websites, networking events, public speaking engagements, and professional relationships. No, you don't need to do all these things. You do, however, need to show up where your target audience has a chance of seeing you. To serve and be seen by the people you are looking to connect with, you must join them where they are.

The Steps of Personal Branding

Personal branding is a process. It is important to begin at the most advantageous place—self-awareness. Most of us are so close to our personal brand we lack real perspective on how others perceive us. In fact, if we're honest, we aren't sure we can even see ourselves clearly either. Getting that perspective is a critical first step in enhancing or establishing any brand. We will cover each step in the following process in greater detail later in this book. But to begin, let's just get an overview of what the process looks like, and why each step is important, as well as why they are in this necessary order.

Self-Reflection and Assessment: Start by reflecting on your current personal brand and identifying areas that you want to change or improve. Consider your values, strengths, skills, and the image you want to project. Assess your current online presence, including social media profiles and any existing personal branding efforts, to understand how you are currently perceived.

Define Your New Brand Identity: Determine how you want to be perceived moving forward. Identify your target audience, the values you want to embody, and the unique qualities and expertise you bring to the table. Define your personal brand story and messaging, highlighting the aspects you want to emphasize in your rebrand.

Research and Inspiration: Conduct research in your desired industry or field to understand current trends, successful personal brands, and the expectations of your target audience. Look for you who have achieved the kind of rebranding or transformation you are seeking and draw inspiration from your journeys.

Online Presence Audit and Optimization: Evaluate your existing online presence and identify areas that need improvement. Update and optimize your social media profiles to align with your new brand identity. Consider creating or updating your personal website to showcase your rebranded self and share relevant content.

Develop Content Strategy: Create a content strategy that supports your rebranding efforts. Determine the types of content you will create and share to reinforce your new personal brand. This can include blog posts, articles, videos, podcasts, or social media updates. Ensure that your content aligns with your brand messaging and resonates with your target audience.

Network and Build Relationships: Engage in networking activities to expand your professional connections and build relationships with you who align with your new brand identity. Attend industry events, join relevant professional groups, and seek opportunities to collaborate or contribute your expertise. Building a strong network can help reinforce your rebranding efforts and open doors for new opportunities.

Consistency and Persistence: Rebranding takes time and consistent effort. Stay committed to your new brand identity and messaging, both online and offline. Be patient with the process and continue to refine and adapt your approach as needed. Consistency and persistence will help solidify your rebrand and create a lasting impression.

Seek Feedback and Iterate: Throughout the rebranding process, seek feedback from trusted you, mentors, or industry professionals. Listen to your insights and perspectives on your new brand identity. Use this feedback to refine your approach and make necessary adjustments.

Remember, rebranding is a gradual process, and it may take time to fully establish and embody your new personal brand. Be patient, stay true to your values and goals, and remain consistent in your efforts to create the desired perception and reputation for yourself.

Getting Help

Personal branding is a vulnerable, often complex, and high-stakes process that may leave you unsure you want to venture into the deep end alone. In fact, many top executives and the companies they represent will hire a personal branding agency to guide them through the process for maximum speed and optimal impact. These agencies approach personal branding by providing strategic guidance, expertise, and support before, during and after a brand is launched. This has a price, of course. Branding agencies, like mine, and many others, provide services that align with the steps of the branding process, and they are, in general, as follows:

Discovery and Assessment: Personal branding agencies typically start by conducting an in-depth discovery process with your clients. This involves understanding the client's goals, values, strengths, target audience, and current brand perception. They may use assessments, interviews, and questionnaires to gather relevant information.

Brand Strategy Development: Based on the information gathered, personal branding agencies work with clients to develop a comprehensive brand strategy. This includes defining the client's unique value proposition, positioning in the market, key messaging, and brand attributes. They help clients identify your target audience and develop strategies to effectively reach and engage with them.

Online Presence and Content Strategy: Agencies assist clients in optimizing your online presence, including social media profiles, personal websites, and other digital platforms. They help clients develop a content strategy that aligns with your brand messaging and target audience. This may involve content creation, curation, and distribution strategies to establish the client's expertise and thought leadership.

Visual Branding and Design: Personal branding agencies often provide guidance on visual branding elements such as logos, color schemes, typography, and overall design aesthetic. They ensure that the visual components of the personal brand align with the desired brand identity and resonate with the target audience.

Personal Branding Collateral: Agencies may help clients develop various personal branding collateral such as business cards, resumes, bios, professional headshots, and presentation templates. These materials are designed to consistently represent the client's personal brand across different touchpoints.

Online Reputation Management: Personal branding agencies assist clients in managing your online reputation and monitoring your digital footprint. They provide guidance on maintaining a positive online presence, managing social media interactions, and addressing any potential reputation issues that may arise.

Thought Leadership and PR Opportunities: Agencies often help clients position themselves as thought leaders in your industry or field. They identify opportunities for clients to showcase your expertise through speaking engagements, guest blogging, media interviews, podcast appearances, and other public relations activities.

Ongoing Brand Monitoring and Evaluation: Personal branding agencies support clients in monitoring and evaluating the effectiveness of your personal branding efforts. They track key metrics, gather feedback from the target audience, and make necessary adjustments to the brand strategy and execution.

If you hire an agency or individual to support your personal branding journey, and even accelerate its success, look for one who will provide comprehensive guidance and support throughout the personal branding journey, leveraging your expertise and industry knowledge to help you build and manage strong personal brands.

Whether you know you want expert help such as one of these agencies like mine provide, or are equally certain you want to make your personal brand a DIY exercise, this book will help you to understand what needs to be done, how to do it, and how much time you will need to invest to accomplish it. You will be a personal branding expert and an informed buyer, no matter which avenue you elect to take.

CHAPTER 3

Meet the Real You

We all want to belong. We also want to be seen, understood and to matter. As a result, most of us spend a great deal of effort learning to read and respond to other people's needs, opinions, and desires. At the same time there are people who have access to the things, both material and intangible, that we crave. We work to appeal to them, in order to access those things, and to gain recognition and rewards from them. Face it – we need other people. This natural, other-centric focus helps us gain clients, advance our careers and woo romantic partners. The ability to connect, convince and convert others is a powerful skill to hone when it is at its highest form of empathy, compassion and collaboration. However, it is not where we must begin when we are re-inventing our own brand. Quite the reverse. We begin by taking a long, unflinching look at ourselves.

We begin with self-reflection—which, candidly, is not everyone's cup of tea. *Surely we don't need to spend a bunch of time contemplating our navels with all this self-awareness mumbo-jumbo, do we?* Yes, my friend. **We d,o** if we're going to build you an effective brand, that is. To get something other than what you have always gotten, you can be certain you must do something other than what you have always done. Even if you are familiar with self-reflection, it's time to dig a little deeper than your usual efforts.

So, let's clear up what gets between us and real self-reflection before we begin, so you can recognize these internal blocks when they come up.

The first bogey is simply fear of unpleasant emotions. It is absolutely true that self-reflection can bring up uncomfortable emotions and thoughts. Some people may fear confronting negative aspects of themselves or facing past mistakes, leading them to avoid introspection to prevent experiencing emotional discomfort. If this sounds like it might be you, then be gentle with yourself. You are not weak or broken if there's some old issues lurking under the surface. In fact, you are very human. You don't need to pick at the scab. When you bump into these issues, be aware of them, and then allow yourself to explore other, more positive avenues for growth first and foremost. This isn't denial. It is actually awareness without self-harm.

Next, you don't know what you don't know. A study by IO psychologist Tasha Eurich found that 95% of people think they're self-aware, but that only 10 to 15% really are. Although the study scientifically links self-aware people with better performance, more promotions, and leading more effectively, some of us are still not aware of the benefits of self-reflection, or may not have developed the habit of introspection. They may not understand how self-reflection can contribute to personal growth, emotional well-being, and better decision-making.

Then there are the twin bogeys of competing time and priorities: In today's fast-paced world, it's almost impossible for most of us not to feel overwhelmed with responsibilities, work, and daily routines, leaving little time or mental space for self-reflection. Internal time spent on personal development can be seen as a non-essential activity, especially when there are pressing external demands.

Speaking of external demands, there are also infinitely possible external distractions: The constant availability of digital devices, social media, and entertainment options can serve as distractions and make it challenging to focus on self-reflection. These distractions can prevent you from dedicating uninterrupted time to introspection. And they seem so very real, compared to the intangible quality of our inner world.

But let's not forget the bogey of our general resistance to change: engaging in self-reflection may lead to the recognition of areas for growth—and that means change is needed. However, some of you may resist change and prefer to maintain your current beliefs, habits, and behaviors, avoiding self-reflection to avoid challenging your existing worldview.

Lastly, cultural or societal norms and expectations can influence your attitude towards self-reflection, even though you may think you are impervious. In some cultures (and let's not forget, there are *generational* cultures too!), introspection may be less emphasized or considered unnecessary, while other cultures may place greater importance on collective identity, or external motivations, rather than individual self-reflection.

Regardless which, if any, of these bogeys might creep up on you, self-reflection is foundational for building a personal brand that is 100%, undeniably you, and designed to take you where you want to go. But where do you begin? You don't need to journey into the mountains so you can sit undisturbed in hours of mantras and meditation.

To begin the process of self-reflection, you can follow these steps:

1. **Create a quiet and comfortable space:** Find a peaceful environment where you can focus without distractions. It could be a room in your home, a park, or any place where you feel calm and at ease.

2. **Set aside dedicated time:** Allocate a specific period, whether it's 15 minutes or an hour, to engage in self-reflection. Consistency is key, so try to establish a routine and make it a regular practice. I recommend daily, although many individuals struggle with even 15 minutes daily at first, if this is a new practice. So, if you must, start with a weekly practice, and gradually increase this sacred time.

3. **Relax and clear your mind:** Take a few deep breaths to relax your body and clear your mind of any clutter. Let go of any immediate concerns or stresses and allow yourself to be present in the moment. One of the easiest ways to become truly present is to focus on your physical sensations, such as observing your breath, or noticing and appreciating an object, such as a candle or plant, in your immediate surroundings.

4. **Ask yourself brand-centric questions:** Begin by asking yourself open-ended questions that encourage deeper thought and introspection. My website provides worksheets and workbooks for digging deeper into many of these questions at StaceyRuth-Says.com/tools. Some examples include:

   - What are my core values and beliefs?
   - What are my strengths and weaknesses?
   - What are my passions and goals in life?
   - What makes me happy or fulfilled?
   - What patterns or habits do I need to address?
   - What are my fears or insecurities?

5. **Reflect on your experiences:** Recollect recent experiences or events and explore how they made you feel and why. Consider both positive and negative experiences and try to identify any lessons or insights you gained from them. Your individual experiences, and how you felt about them are a remarkable guide to some of the essential attributes of your personal brand.

6. **Write in a journal:** Consider keeping a journal dedicated to self-reflection. Write down your thoughts, emotions, and observations. The act of writing can help clarify your thinking and provide a record of your journey.

7. **Practice active listening to yourself:** Actively listen to your thoughts, feelings, and emotions without judgment. Pay attention to your intuition and inner voice. Be honest with yourself and strive for self-awareness. This means you don't need to attach to a certain set of thoughts and feelings. You are just observing, as if you were not the person directly involved.

8. **Seek feedback from others:** Engage in conversations with trusted friends, family members, or mentors who can provide valuable insights and perspectives about you. Your observations can help you gain a more well-rounded understanding of yourself. A great exercise is to invite them to tell you the top three

positive attributes they think belong to you, and then the top three areas for improvement they perceive. This is intended, again, to be objective, and if someone is harsh about the latter, they are not the right person to be responding.

9. **Embrace self-compassion:** Self-reflection should be approached with kindness and compassion. Acknowledge your strengths and accomplishments, but also accept your flaws and areas for improvement. Treat yourself with the same empathy you would extend to a dear friend.

10. **Take action and set goals:** Use the insights gained from self-reflection to set meaningful goals and make positive changes in your life. Self-reflection is only valuable if it leads to personal growth and transformation.

Remember that self-reflection is an ongoing process, and it may take time to develop the habit and dive deeper into your inner thoughts and perceptions. Be patient with yourself, and allow the process to unfold naturally. Remember, if you have not done this sort of work to a great degree in the past, you might feel awkward or unsure. Don't try to force brilliant inspirations to appear in the first five minutes. Instead, be willing to become curious and probe at the edges of your consciousness in order to discover what has been there all along.

The Essence of Your Brand

Self-reflection plays a significant role in any leadership role, and that includes self-leadership. It is the biggest key to unlocking the essence of your brand. By committedly engaging in it, you can gain deeper insights into your strengths, weaknesses, values, passions, and goals – which are non-negotiable in personal branding.

The process of self-reflection may take weeks or months, but persistence does pay off here. Sticking it out will help you in pretty much any endeavor, from building a business that serves you, to becoming a better employer, parent or team member. And it is crucial when it comes to developing an authentic and compelling personal brand. If you don't quite understand why you can't skip all the seemingly intangible self-reflection work, here are several ways self-reflection provides necessary insight for personal branding:

Clarifying personal values: Self-reflection allows you to identify and understand your core values. We all have them. By aligning your personal brand with these values, they can build a genuine and consistent image that resonates with your target audience. The only way to know them with confidence is to go digging within yourself. These values are, after all, about *you*, not your clients or your audience.

Discovering strengths and weaknesses: Self-reflection helps you recognize your strengths and weaknesses, enabling you to emphasize your unique abilities and expertise in your personal brand. By understanding your limitations, you can work on improving your image to focus on strengths first and foremost, while seeking opportunities for improving on those areas of growth. I don't know many people who love looking at their weaknesses (although there are a handful who seem to get some perverse delight out of beating themselves up over their shortcomings). However, when we admit areas for improvement, without all the self-recrimination for our imperfections, we are finally able to affect change. Self-reflection shows this faster and more effectively than any strengths finder I've ever found. And doing so allows us to promote our personal brand's strengths accurately, while we are hard at work behind the scenes turning those same weaknesses into strengths—or at least minimizing them.

Identifying passions and interests: Self-reflection helps you identify your true passions and interests. Sadly, too many of us have adopted passions and interests out of convenience or to meet other people's idea of success before our own. But if we don't do the work to understand our own inner motivations, our brand will remain very surface and provide little appeal. When incorporated into personal branding, these elements can add authenticity and enthusiasm to your overall image, making them more relatable and engaging to others.

Defining a clear vision and goals: Self-reflection allows you to establish a clear vision for your personal brand. By setting specific goals and objectives, they can develop a focused strategy to build your brand identity, establish your expertise, and achieve long-term success. If you find yourself tempted to set goals and objectives for your brand in order to get other people's approval, or meet some mark of success that society promotes, then a little more individuality might be in order. Go within and check those automatic goals against what really lights you up.

Building self-confidence: Through self-reflection, you can develop a better understanding of your accomplishments, experiences, and unique qualities. This enhanced self-awareness contributes to increased self-confidence, which is vital for effective personal branding.

Enhancing authenticity: Authenticity is crucial in personal branding. I cannot say that enough, given the pervasive cultural belief in branding's inauthenticity. By engaging in self-reflection, you can uncover your true self, aligning your personal brand with your genuine identity. This authenticity creates trust and builds stronger connections with your audience. No matter how carefully crafted, a false brand presence emits clues to its subterfuge. While people may not know why something feels "off" they will still feel it, and hold their distance.

Evaluating and adapting: Self-reflection allows you to assess your personal brand periodically. By evaluating your progress, gathering feedback, and reflecting on your experiences, they can make necessary adjustments and refine your brand to ensure it remains relevant and impactful.

In summary, self-reflection helps you develop a strong personal brand by providing clarity, authenticity, self-awareness, and a solid foundation for effective communication and engagement with your audience. By understanding themselves deeply, you can effectively showcase your unique qualities and expertise, differentiate themselves from others, and build a memorable personal brand that resonates with your desired goals and values.

The Evolution of Your Brand

Everyone has a brand. This book is not about building your brand from scratch, since, inevitably your brand is already a work in process. It is the current summation of all your qualities and experiences to-date. And, just like you, the individual, your brand will not and cannot remain static and unchanging. You evolve over time. And your brand evolves right along with you. The most successful personal brands are built around this concept, leveraging brand evolution consciously, with deep intentionality.

The reason evolution matters so greatly is this: personal brands, like any other aspect of life, must evolve in order to stay relevant and effective in a changing world. As society, technology, and cultural trends evolve, personal branding strategies must adapt to meet the demands of the times.

Personal brands have traditionally focused on establishing a unique identity and showcasing expertise. While these aspects remain important, modern personal brands must also emphasize authenticity and purpose. People are increasingly drawn to individuals who are genuine, transparent, and aligned with a meaningful mission or values. Evolving personal brands should strive to communicate a sense of purpose and showcase authentic qualities that resonate with their audience.

Similarly, with the rapid advancement of technology and the proliferation of social media platforms, your personal brand must adapt to the changing landscape of online presence. It is no longer enough to focus solely on one platform. Although technically, you aren't obligated to build an online presence in order to build your personal brand, doing so increases your influence more rapidly. Although this book won't make online branding its core focus, it is important to note that successful personal brands typically have a multi-platform strategy that extends across various social media channels, websites, podcasts, video content, and more. This allows individuals to reach and engage with a broader audience while catering to different preferences and demographics. This is one of the fastest evolving areas for personal branding, and your brand must weigh carefully how you want to present yourself, and where.

Online notwithstanding, in today's fast-paced world, personal brands must embrace a mindset of continuous learning and adaptability. Staying updated with industry trends, acquiring new skills, and being open to change are vital for personal brand evolution. This may involve attending conferences, participating in online courses, or actively seeking out opportunities to grow and expand knowledge. By staying ahead of the curve and adapting to new technologies and methodologies, you can remain relevant and valuable to your audience.

Not to harp on the digital media, but video and visual content have become dominant forms of communication in the digital landscape. Personal brands must adapt by incorporating these formats into their strategies. Platforms like YouTube, Instagram, TikTok, and LinkedIn provide opportunities to share engaging video content that showcases personality, expertise, and storytelling. Embrace some, most or all of these mediums and investing in high-quality visual content creation to capture the attention and interest of your audience is becoming a price of entry for growing your brand.

Additionally, the traditional growth channels, such as collaborations and partnerships, remain essential for personal brand growth. Engaging with other individuals, brands, or influencers in complementary fields can expand reach, foster new connections, and provide opportunities for cross-promotion. Collaborative efforts can include joint content creation, co-hosting events or webinars, or even launching products or services together. Such alliances can help personal brands evolve by tapping into new audiences and leveraging collective expertise.

Also worth mentioning here, is that in an era of increasing concern for social and environmental issues, personal brands benefit greatly by demonstrating a commitment to social impact and sustainability. Evolving personal brands who align themselves with causes that resonate with their values, purpose and goals are quickly able to grow their visibility through a synergy in an existing, larger conversation. By showcasing their dedication to making a positive difference in the world, personal brands can attract like-minded individuals and demonstrate a genuine concern for global challenges. These topics ad challenges change quickly, so it is less important to try and be "trendy" and more important to be passionate about these allegiances.

The real you is infinitely worth discovering, and maintaining a deep connection with. Some days will be more self-aware than others. However, when you are able to maintain that connection pretty regularly, it is simply easier to evolve to keep pace with the ever-changing landscape of technology, society, and cultural trends. By emphasizing authenticity, multi-platform presence, continuous learning, collaboration, visual content, and social impact, you and your brand can adapt and thrive in an increasingly dynamic world.

CHAPTER 4

Values, Vision & Vigor

Everything begins with your values. That's a big idea to get one's head around. So, I will spell it out a little more: values are your one-of-a-kind, signature vibrational frequency. They act as guiding principles that help you make decisions and navigate life. What's more, our values can play a significant role in attracting relationships and opportunities in several ways:

When our true values align with those of our clients, employers/employees or potential partners, it creates a sense of resonance and connection. This is true even when the values are not explicitly stated by either party. This happens as we live and operate in accordance with them. As such, these implicit or explicit shared values can build trust, enhance rapport, and foster a deeper understanding between parties. Others who resonate with our values are more likely to be attracted to our offerings and want to work with us.

Clearly expressing our values allows us to showcase our authenticity (yes, you will get tired of this word before the end of this book, so I will beg your forgiveness now). In a crowded marketplace, having a distinct set of values can differentiate us from competitors and attract clients who value what we stand for. It is a foundational principle of marketing as well as corporate branding, that we are inexorably drawn to individuals or organizations that demonstrate consistency, transparency, and a strong sense of purpose rooted in their values.

When you are living and operating in alignment with your values, it is easier to enhance your reputation. Positive word-of-mouth referrals can lead to a steady stream of opportunities, as people are inclined to recommend those who share their values.

Our values serve as a magnet for like-minded individuals. When we embody and promote our values, we naturally attract people who share similar beliefs and principles. This can lead to the formation of a supportive community, networking opportunities, and collaborations that align with our goals and values. This translates directly to business, where clients and partners often seek relationships with organizations that align with their cultural values. When our values align with the values of our target audience, it increases the likelihood of developing long-term relationships and fostering loyalty. Clients who feel a strong alignment with our values are more likely to stay engaged, refer others, and become repeat customers.

If you are leading an organization, your personal values have a direct impact on your organization's values as well. Values-driven organizations have stronger brand identities, since just like personal branding, their brand begins with understanding their values.

By clearly communicating your values through your brand vision, purpose, message, and—where applicable—marketing efforts, you can attract clients and opportunities that resonate with your brand. A compelling narrative rooted in values can inspire individuals to engage with your offerings and support your mission.

When you live your values and make them known, you will, with surprising frequency, attract opportunities that align with those values. This can manifest as partnerships, collaborations, speaking engagements, or projects that are in line with your core beliefs.

By staying true to your values, you create an energetic magnet that draws in opportunities that align with who you are and what you stand for. If this sounds too woo-woo for you, here's the principle at play: your self-awareness of your values helps you identify more readily the opportunities and people that are best able to move you forward toward your goals and purpose. That's all there is to it. That's a massive impact from a small investment in your awareness!

Finding Your Personal Values

If you are with me about the power of personal values for your personal brand at this point, you are likely asking yourself exactly how do you identify those values with any degree of certainty. That is the subject of much debate, and there are endless theories about how to uncover them, how many to focus on, and how variable they are through that ongoing evolution we discussed in the last chapter.

I will share with you my approach, which I believe is as good as any other approach out there, and better than most. But before I do, I want to clear up one little sticking point I often run across at this point with some of my coaching clients. That is, precisely what values are we looking for here?

We aren't talking about family values here, like love and honesty. Nor are we talking about business differentiators such as customer service, or innovation. Those words might be in your list of personal values, but they don't have to be. You might value other things more, which is what make you utterly unique. Your values are beyond reproach, and you most likely have scores of them. What we are looking for when we go digging for those that represent you and your brand most powerfully are the ones that are strongest. I encourage you to narrow them to three to four. Some suggest six. Others say no more than two. So, I'll give you some leeway to find the final number you will include. Regardless, here is the process I use with my clients, which you already began through self-reflection in the last chapter. I have a *Values Worksheet* with the following steps that you can access here: https://www.staceyruthsays.com/tools

The search to identify your personal values is a multi-faceted process that involves looking both inward and outward. It is meant to be fun and inspiring, so try to enjoy the work if you can.

1) **Begin with External Feedback:**

   - Seek feedback from trusted friends, family members, or mentors. Ask them to share their observations about your character, strengths, and what they admire about you. If they can condense their reflections to one word be concept, such as "honest" or "creative," that would be ideal.

- Pay attention to recurring themes or qualities mentioned by others. Note the values they associate with you and consider whether they resonate with you as well.

2. **Examine Your Priorities:**

- Reflect on your priorities in life, which, like it or not, show up where you spend most of your time. What are the things that matter most to you? Consider areas such as family, career, health, personal growth, relationships, community, and spirituality.

- Evaluate how you allocate your time, energy, and resources. Your priorities often reflect your values, so think about what you invest the most in and why.

3. **Capture Your Heroes' Qualities:**

- Think about people you admire and consider them as your heroes or role models. Identify the qualities and values they possess that inspire you.

- Reflect on why you admire them and how their values align with your own aspirations. Consider incorporating those values into your own value system.

4. **Explore The Essence of Your Enjoyable Past Times:**

- Recall moments or activities in your life when you felt truly fulfilled, engaged, or content. Those are the moments when time stood still. What values were present during those experiences?

- Consider the activities, relationships, or environments that made those moments special. Identify the underlying values that were being honored or expressed.

5. **Envision Several Best Day Scenarios:**

- Visualize your ideal or "best" day scenarios across different areas of your life. Imagine a day where everything goes perfectly and aligns with your desires and aspirations.
- Reflect on the experiences, feelings, and values present in those scenarios. Identify the core values that underpin your sense of fulfillment and happiness.

6. **Claim Your Passions:**

- Explore your passions and interests. What activities or causes energize you, bring you joy, or make you feel fully alive?
- Consider the values that drive your passions. For example, if you are passionate about environmental sustainability, the underlying values might include environmental stewardship, responsibility, and a desire for a better future.

7. **Reflection and Integration:**

- Review all the information you have gathered from external feedback, priorities, heroes' qualities, enjoyable past times, best day scenarios, and passions.
- Look for common themes, overlapping values, or patterns that emerge. Pay attention to values that consistently resonate with you across different contexts.
- Create a list of your identified values and prioritize them based on their importance to you. Be open to refining and revising this list as you gain further clarity and self-awareness.

Once you've mined these areas for insight, you ought to have a fairly good idea of what some of your values actually are. In fact, you probably have too many to be really manageable on your list. To assist you in identifying some inspiring values words, I have included a list in the *Values Worksheet*. This list is not intended to be all-inclusive, but at over 300 words, it should get you going. So, go ahead, and start digging. Make yourself a big, delicious list. Then it's time to begin the next phase of the process—refining.

Prioritize your values: When you have a list of ten or twelve values, review and prioritize them. Look for patterns or similarities among your values.

Consider which values feel most essential and non-negotiable to you. You can prioritize them by numbering or ranking them based on their importance to you.

Reflect on conflicts: Reflect on any conflicts or dilemmas you've experienced in the past. Think about situations where you felt torn or faced difficult decisions. Consider the values that were in conflict during those times. This reflection can help you gain deeper insight into your values and understand their significance and deep influence on your emotions and decisions, as well as your behavior.

Test your values: Put your values to the test in real-life situations. Observe how your values guide your actions and decisions. Notice the feelings of fulfillment or misalignment that arise when you live according to or against your values. This practical testing will help you refine and solidify your understanding of your personal values.

Refine and revise: Personal values can evolve over time as you gain new experiences and perspectives. Continuously review and refine your values to ensure they still align with your authentic self. Be open to updating and revising your values as needed.

Your Brand 's Foundation: The Mission, Vision and Purpose

Brand mission, vision, and purpose are distinct concepts within personal brand strategy. Each serves a specific role which is vital to moving your brand forward. Unfortunately, for the uninitiated, your mission, vision and purpose can easily be confused with one another, and amid the confusion, they can get skipped in the branding process.

I don't understand my mission, vision or purpose, so it must not be that important!

If you are thinking that, let me encourage you to not be so hasty to pass them off as some sort of window dressing. Instead, I hope you can come to understand that they become your necessary guiding principles and north star of whether opportunities that come your way are right for you, or need to be left alone in favor of the ones that truly are. Let's take a look at each of these ideas very briefly, and get clear about their importance and the interconnection between them. Then we'll look at how to craft yours from your values.

Brand Mission: The brand mission is a concise statement that describes the brand's current activities, target audience, and the value it provides. It outlines what the brand does and how it serves its customers. In just a few words—preferably one, short, pithy sentence—it provides high-level guidance for day-to-day operations, decision-making, and strategic initiatives. The mission statement helps align the brand's activities with its overall objectives.

Brand Vision: By contrast, the brand vision represents a long-term, aspirational goal or desired future state that the brand aims to achieve. It defines where the brand wants to be in the future and provides a sense of direction for growth and development. For instance, if you want to become the go-to organization in your field, or become the CEO of a company you admire, these are visions worth pursuing. The vision is forward-looking and articulates the brand's overarching purpose, aspirations, and desired impact on the world. It guides strategic decision-making, inspires innovation, and aligns the brand's activities with its long-term goals. (It is worth mentioning here that goals and objectives are not the same either. Goals are broader, while objectives are specific and measurable.)

Brand Purpose: Brand purpose is the fundamental reason why a brand exists beyond making a profit. It embodies the brand's core values, beliefs, and the positive impact it seeks to have on society or its target audience. The purpose goes beyond the brand's products or services and provides a sense of meaning. It helps establish an emotional connection with customers and stakeholders and defines the brand's role in addressing societal or environmental challenges.

Your brand purpose provides the foundation for your brand by defining its fundamental reason for existence and its positive impact on the world. Meanwhile your brand vision represents the desired future state, inspired by the purpose, that you aim to achieve over the long term. Bringing it together, your brand mission outlines your needed current activities and serves as a roadmap to fulfill the purpose and move closer to the vision. Voila!

The brand purpose serves as the guiding principle that informs both the brand vision and mission. The purpose provides the "why" for the brand, while the vision and mission provide the "what" and "how" respectively. The vision sets the long-term direction, while the mission outlines the immediate actions to be taken.

Each of these concepts contribute to a strong brand strategy. They you're your brand's skeletal structure. While your brand purpose provides meaning and guides its strategic decision-making, helping it resonate with customers and stakeholders, your vision creates a clear future direction, inspiring and aligning all your activities and initiatives. Then your brand mission is able to guide your day-to-day actions and more granular decision-making, ensuring that you are delivering on your stated purpose and vision.

When all three elements work together harmoniously, they create a strong and cohesive personal brand identity, driving greater appeal and impact for you, where you desire it most.

Values play a crucial role in defining your brand's mission, vision, and purpose, for the same reasons we need those values in the first place. If your mission, vision and purpose are the brand skeleton, values are the DNA.

If you begin building your mission, vision or purpose statement without including your values words, I would question how important those values actually are to you! Let your brand be a living thing. That means you will want to avoid trying to sound so sophisticated and professional that you lose the essential emotional qualities a brand must have to create meaningful appeal. Dull corporate mission statements are the laughing stock of the business world. Don't get lured into that trap. Keep it fresh. Keep it real.

Creating Your Purpose Statement

As with most things branding, there is no single right or wrong way to create your purpose, mission or vision statements. There are, however, generally accepted best practices, and we'll use those as our guides. The first guideline is that the most effective order for your three foundational personal brand statements are 1) purpose, then 2) mission and lastly, 3) vision. So we will begin with your purpose statement.

A personal brand purpose statement is a concise and impactful declaration that communicates the essence of your personal brand and the reason behind your work or existence. It helps define your values, mission, and the unique contribution you strive to make in your field or industry. While the exact format may vary depending on your preferences and context, here's a general guideline you can follow to create an effective personal brand purpose statement.

Ultimately, you will want to condense each of these statements to the shortest most essential qualities for ease and inspiration, like Nike's *Just Do It*. Or Honda's *Be the company the world wants to exist*. (Now that's audacious!) But to begin with, in the ideation process, allow yourself the grace to use more words before you try to condense it all into award-winning marketing headlines.

Start with an introductory phrase. Begin your statement by introducing yourself or stating your name. For example, "I am [Your Name]" or "I am a [Your Role]."

Next express your passion and values. Clearly articulate the area or industry that you're passionate about and the specific aspect of it that drives you. Additionally, highlight the core values that guide your work. This showcases your genuine enthusiasm and the principles that underpin your personal brand. For example, *I am passionate about helping small business succeed through effective leadership and strategy, because there is an enormous leadership gap in our global culture which must be addressed. My values are boldness, creativity and curiosity, which form the approach I uniquely bring to this effort.*

Once you have clarity on your passion and values, you are ready to define your unique contribution: Emphasize the specific impact or change you aspire to make within your field or industry. Focus on the value you aim to bring and how it aligns with your passion and values. This highlights the unique contribution you offer.

Once you have these distinct components in place, summarize for real impact. Refine and condense your purpose statement by summarizing the disparate pieces with clarity. Ensure your end product statement reflects the "why" behind your personal brand, resonates with your values, and communicates your deep-seated purpose. For example:

"I am [Your Name], passionately dedicated to [area/industry]. Guided by [core values], my purpose is to [verb] [target audience/industry] by [specific contribution], driven by the belief that [belief or conviction]."

Customize this format by filling in the brackets with your own specific details.

"I am Stacey Ruth, passionately dedicated to activating great business leaders using meaningful strategies and innovative thinking. Guided by boldness, creativity and curiosity, my purpose is to end the leadership gap, knowing that small business success drives our culture's sustainability."

Remember, the purpose statement should convey the "why" behind your personal brand and capture the essence of your values, passions, and the unique contribution you strive to make. Take time to reflect on your core motivations and refine your purpose statement until it accurately represents the driving force behind your personal brand.

Creating Your Mission Statement

Once you have a personal brand mission statement in hand, it's time to tackle your personal brand mission statement, which is is more action-oriented and specific. A mission statement outlines the goals, objectives, and strategies you will employ to achieve your purpose. See how that works?

It clarifies the target audience you aim to serve, the problem you address, your unique approach or solution, and the desired impact or outcome. The mission statement provides a clear roadmap and direction for your personal brand's activities and initiatives. Try not to overthink this. It doesn't need to be a Nobel Prize-winning statement. It just needs to create your roadmap forward.

Start with an introductory phrase: Begin your statement by introducing yourself or stating your name. For example, "I am [Your Name]" or "My name is [Your Name]."

Then identify your target audience: Clearly define the specific group or audience you aim to serve or impact through your personal brand. This helps focus your mission statement and tailor your efforts. I have created the Ideal Customer Worksheet, to help you do that, located at www.insideoutsmart.com/ideal-customer-worksheet. Keep in mind, you want to narrow your audience, so it is specific enough to appeal to someone. Women, for example is too broad. Executive women in technology, or women who are leaving a corporate job to start a business, are much closer to the mark. You can get even more narrow, if you like, and remember you will have more than one ideal customer.

Now that you know who you are helping, state the problem or need that they are aware of. Keep in mind it is tempting to want to tell them about the real problem they have which you can solve, such as a lack of strategy, but that will fall on deaf ears, if what they are experiencing is pure overwhelm or lack of business in the pipeline. So, meet them where they are, with the problem they already know about. You can help them solve the root problem later. Articulate that main challenge, problem, or need that your target audience has awareness of. This provides context and highlights the gap you aim to fill.

Once you have the previous steps in place, describe your unique approach or solution. Explain how you plan to address the identified problem or need in a distinctive and effective manner. Emphasize the unique qualities, skills, or expertise that set you apart and contribute to your approach or solution.

So, what is the result? Outline the desired impact or outcome in vivid, emotionally loaded terms. Clearly articulate the positive change or impact you strive to create through your personal brand's activities. This should demonstrate the ultimate goal or transformation you want to facilitate within your target audience.

Lastly, summarize with clarity and purpose everything you just captured. Craft a concise statement that encompasses the above elements and reflects your personal brand's mission. Make sure it aligns with your purpose and conveys the specific actions and strategies you will employ. Customize the format with your own details. For example:

"My personal brand mission is to [verb] [target audience] by [unique approach/solution] to [desired impact/outcome]."

Customize this format to fit your personal brand's unique mission and goals.

Creating Your Vision Statement

Once you have a mission and purpose statement, your vision statement can complement and expand upon them by providing a broader and aspirational view of your desired future state. Usually, this vision is inclusive of both you, and the audience you are serving. Here's a broad approach for structuring a vision statement that aligns with an existing mission and purpose:

Start with an inspiring opening. Begin your vision statement with an attention-grabbing sentence that sparks enthusiasm and creates a sense of excitement about the future you envision. This statement will become the shorthand version of your vision statement for you to remember and use frequently.

Reiterate your mission and purpose: Briefly summarize your existing mission and purpose statement to provide context and continuity. Remind yourself and your audience of the overall direction and values that guide your actions.

Then paint a vivid picture of the future. Use descriptive and imaginative language to articulate a compelling vision of what you aspire to achieve. Describe the ideal state or outcomes you envision for yourself, your brand, and the impact you want to have on others.

Next, it's good to expand on your goals and aspirations. Elaborate on them by focusing on the specific milestones or achievements you hope to reach. Clearly communicate the significance and positive change these accomplishments will bring. This is where you go big. If there's a part of you that shrinks from being specific and putting on paper something that you are not 100% confident you can achieve, this would be a great point to confront that voice. If it is allowed to call the shots, you and your brand will continue to play small. I find it helpful to give myself permission to think in bold, audacious outcomes, and focus less on whether I have reached them, and more on what will continue to move me towards them.

When you have captured those big goals, briefly emphasize your unique approach. Highlight the distinctive qualities, approaches, or values that set you apart from others in pursuing your mission and vision. Showcase how your unique perspective will contribute to your success and the value you will bring to your audience.

Speaking of your audience, the vision statement in its complete form is designed to connect with them. Add some language to demonstrate how your vision aligns with the needs, desires, or aspirations of your target audience. Show them how your brand and future achievements will positively impact and resonate with them.

Finally, conclude your vision statement with a call to action. Wrap up your vision statement by inspiring and motivating your audience to engage with your personal brand and join you on your journey. Encourage them to support and be part of the realization of your vision. This is the essence of leadership.

Remember, this structure is a guideline, and you should adapt it to suit your own personal brand and existing mission and purpose statements. Ensure that your vision statement remains aligned with your overall brand narrative and communicates a clear and compelling vision for your future.

Here are a couple of examples of vision statements that complement existing mission and purpose statements:

Example 1:

Mission Statement: To innovatively provide affordable and accessible education to underserved communities.

Purpose Statement: Boldly empowering individuals through education to create a brighter future.

Vision Statement: Our vision is to create a world where education knows no boundaries. We envision a future where every individual, regardless of their background or socioeconomic status, has equal access to high-quality education. Through our innovative programs and partnerships, we aim to break down barriers and empower communities to thrive. Together, we will build a society where education is a transformative force that unlocks limitless opportunities for all.

Example 2:

Mission Statement: To revolutionize the way people connect and communicate across the globe.

Purpose Statement: Enabling meaningful connections to bridge distances and foster understanding.

Vision Statement: Our vision is a connected world, where borders cease to exist and understanding flourishes. We imagine a future where our advanced communication technologies bring people together, transcending geographical and cultural barriers. Through our relentless pursuit of innovation and collaboration, we aim to create a global community that embraces diversity and embraces shared values. Together, we will redefine the way we connect, fostering empathy, collaboration, and positive change for generations to come.

These examples showcase how the vision statements build upon the mission and purpose statements, providing a broader and aspirational view of the desired future state. They communicate a compelling vision, evoke emotions, and inspire others to join in the pursuit of those visions. Your values words can be directly present, or implied at this point. In either case, you use them as the springboard.

Your Strength. Your Power.

Like your values, your personal strengths are unique to you. This is the source of your personal brand's vigor, as the title of this chapter implies. If everyone had the same strengths, we would find every endeavor, team and process very lopsided. As a matter of fact, there are many different ways to assess your strengths in many different contexts., and there are online assessments for each of them.

You may want to explore these, and others, as you reflect on what your unique strengths actually are.

Personality assessments: These assessments, such as the Myers-Briggs Type Indicator (MBTI) or the Big Five Personality Traits, measure different dimensions of personality. By understanding your personality traits, you can gain insights into your natural tendencies, preferences, and strengths. For example, extroversion may indicate strengths in social interaction and leadership, while conscientiousness may reflect strengths in organization and attention to detail.

Strengths-based assessments: The CliftonStrengths assessment (formerly StrengthsFinder) is a popular tool that identifies an individual's top strengths out of a list of 34 themes. It helps uncover areas where you have a natural talent and can excel. By focusing on these strengths, you can leverage them to enhance your personal brand and achieve success in your chosen endeavors.

Skills assessments: Skills assessments evaluate an individual's specific abilities or competencies. They can be job-specific or more general. For example, computer programming skills, language proficiency tests, or problem-solving assessments measure specific skills and abilities. By identifying your areas of proficiency, you can capitalize on them and align them with your personal brand.

Interest inventories: Interest inventories, such as the Holland Codes or Strong Interest Inventory, measure an individual's preferences and interests in various areas, such as careers or hobbies. By understanding your interests, you can uncover areas where you are likely to excel and find fulfillment. These interests can point towards potential strengths to develop and leverage.

Emotional intelligence assessments: Emotional intelligence (EQ) assessments evaluate an individual's ability to recognize, understand, and manage emotions, both in themselves and others. By measuring EQ, these assessments can help identify strengths related to empathy, self-awareness, social skills, and emotional resilience.

It's important to note that assessments provide insights and indications, but they are not definitive or exhaustive measures of personal strengths. They serve as tools to help individuals gain self-awareness and discover areas where they can excel. It's valuable to interpret assessment results in conjunction with self-reflection, feedback from others, and real-life experiences to form a comprehensive understanding of your personal strengths and what to lean into as you are building the impact of your personal brand.

Now comes the spoiler alert: as you uncover your greatest strengths, it is inevitable you will also discover some weaknesses too. Building a strong personal brand is an evolutionary process, that includes excavating the good with the bad. The weaknesses find are there to be addressed by you, not avoided.

Those pesky weaknesses are not fatal flaws. There is a sometimes-irresistible urge to say, "Weaknesses? What weaknesses? Those aren't actual weaknesses. Those are my perfect imperfections." As long as you don't advocate for them remaining as they are, whatever word you want to call them by is fine. However, no matter what you choose to call them, they are your growth edge. By acknowledging your weaknesses and actively working on them, you can create a more authentic and compelling personal brand that aligns with your goals and aspirations.

Here are some of the ways you can continue to address your weaknesses, even as you are presenting your brand and its strengths to the world:

Skill Development: If your weaknesses are related to specific skills, invest time and effort in developing those skills. Enroll in training programs, take relevant courses, read books, or seek mentorship in areas where you need improvement. Developing new skills will not only enhance your personal brand but also boost your confidence.

Leverage Strengths: When you actively focus on leveraging your strengths to compensate for your weaknesses in your brand, you can also use those same strengths to transform weaknesses simultaneously. Emphasize the unique qualities and skills that set you apart and make you valuable to others, then use your strengths on yourself too. Act as if you were your own client or customer, who needed your strengths in order to succeed.

Seek Opportunities for Growth: It might feel a tad uncomfortable, but the best way to overcome weaknesses is through opportunities that challenge you in precisely those areas. This is really what is meant by getting out of your comfort zone. So, if active listening is a weakness for you at present, then during your networking and meeting settings, practice actively listening for certain periods of time before you speak. Practice with family and friends. Practice on phone calls and in retail environments. Practice every time you interact with another person. Embracing these opportunities will enable you to learn, grow, and overcome your weaknesses.

Network and Seek Guidance: By now you have noticed that I promote interpersonal connections as much, or more, than digital ones for personal branding. That's because live interactions provide immediate feedback on how your brand is functioning. Build relationships with professionals in your industry who can provide needed guidance and mentorship to transmute your weaknesses. You cannot get that sort of support easily, if at all, online. Attend industry events, join professional organizations, and engage in networking opportunities to connect with like-minded individuals who can offer perspective and advice on how they might have dealt with those same challenges themselves.

Embrace Continuous Improvement: Since addressing weaknesses is an ongoing process, it is necessary to embrace a growth mindset and commit to self-reinvention. At some point most of us realize that no weakness is really permanent without us co-signing its place of permanence. The buck stops with you. Since you have the ability to improve, and every effort you make in that direction creates incremental improvement, the path through weaknesses can even become enjoyable. Thus, embracing continuous improvement implies it is possible to enjoy the experience.

We are all a work in progress. Our values, vision and strengths grow and evolve over time. The best any of us can do as we are building our personal brand is to create a snapshot of where we find ourselves in this moment, with an eye on the horizon, heading toward where we want to be. If you can embrace this entire effort as a lifelong practice, your brand will be head and shoulders beyond the majority of your peers.

CHAPTER 5

Giving Voice to Your Brand

When you speak, you inevitably communicate more than you say. You communicate your emotional state, your energy level, your inner drivers, and often, you communicate things about yourself and your motivations you may be entirely unaware of. Our work in this chapter is to make as much of that spoken and unspoken content both intentional and self-aware.

When I work with executives as a speech coach, I focus on their cadence, body language and how they are connecting with their audience real-time as much as the words they are speaking. That is the essence of your brand's voice. You already know you must be as authentically yourself as possible. Now it's time to focus on how your words and actions align with the real you.

The Power of Your Spoken and Unspoken Words

Your voice, in its many forms, is a powerful, and often under-used tool. Every interaction, whether it's a keynote address to a room full of industry peer, customers, top executives or a one-on-one conversation with a colleague, is an opportunity to convey your personal brand. Does that mean you need a voice coach? No. Still, taking control of your voice involves several factors that will require practice in order to really put your audible voice to work for you.

We've all heard someone say, "I'm not sure I like your tone!" Or, in a more positive light, "You have a very comforting tone I appreciate."

Tones in communication can vary widely and are often linked to different emotions and intentions. Observe yourself and see how many you can identify using in a given day.

While there isn't a finite list of all possible tones, here is a compilation of some common tones along with how they can be tied to brand personality traits:

- **Enthusiastic:** Associated with energy, positivity, and excitement. It's suitable for brands that want to inspire and motivate their audience.
- **Empathetic:** Reflects understanding, compassion, and a caring attitude. Brands aiming to connect on a personal level and show they genuinely care may use this tone.
- **Confident:** Conveys authority, competence, and self-assuredness. It's often used by brands that want to establish trust and credibility.
- **Serious:** Indicates importance, urgency, and a no-nonsense approach. Brands dealing with critical issues or providing vital services may adopt this tone.
- **Inspirational:** Evokes hope, aspiration, and a sense of purpose. Brands seeking to inspire positive change or personal growth often use this tone.
- **Educational:** Focused on sharing knowledge and expertise. Brands aiming to be seen as experts or thought leaders frequently employ this tone.
- **Casual:** Represents informality, approachability, and a relaxed style. Brands targeting a younger or more laid-back audience may use this tone.
- **Humorous:** Adds humor, wit, and light-heartedness to communication. Brands looking to entertain and create memorable experiences often adopt this tone.

- **Formal:** Exudes professionalism, respect, and seriousness. Brands operating in traditional or conservative industries often use this tone.
- **Empowering:** Encourages action, self-improvement, and personal growth. Brands that want to motivate their audience to take control of their lives may use this tone.
- **Authoritative:** Asserts expertise and dominance in a field. Brands looking to establish themselves as leaders often employ this tone.
- **Inquisitive:** Raises questions and prompts critical thinking. Brands encouraging curiosity and exploration may adopt this tone.
- **Optimistic:** Radiates positivity, hope, and a bright outlook. Brands seeking to associate themselves with optimism and a better future may use this tone.
- **Sincere:** Conveys honesty, authenticity, and transparency. Brands striving to build trust and authenticity often employ this tone.
- **Motivational:** Inspires action, perseverance, and determination. Brands that want to motivate their audience to overcome challenges may use this tone.

These tones are not mutually exclusive, and a brand's communication can incorporate a mixture of tones depending on the context and message. Additionally, the selection of a tone should align with the brand's personality, values, and the emotions it wants to evoke in its audience. Consistency in tone—using the same ones for similar situations—maintains brand identity and build strong connections with whoever your audience is.

Choosing the appropriate tone for your message is a strategic decision. To select the right tone for the impact you desire to achieve, consider the following:

Know Your Audience: Understand the preferences and expectations of your audience. Tailor your tone to resonate with them. If you're speaking to a group of investors, a confident and serious tone may be suitable. For a team-building workshop, an enthusiastic and empathetic tone could be more effective.

Align with Your Brand Values: Ensure that your chosen tone aligns with your personal values and your brand's mission and vision. Authenticity is key to maintaining trust and consistency in your personal brand.

Consider the Message: Analyze the nature of your message. Is it a call to action, an inspirational talk, or a problem-solving discussion? Your tone should match the message's intent.

Practice Self-awareness: Continually monitor your tone, inflection, and cadence. Solicit feedback from trusted colleagues or mentors to ensure your communication style aligns with your desired impact.

Cadence and Rhythm

As you grow your personal brand, opportunities to present in the public eye, from speaking on the stage, to podcast and broadcast interviews will become more prevalent. Your cadence will become much more important and one of the most memorable components of your public facing brand. Your cadence sends subtle messages about your personality, confidence, and engagement. It's a reflection of your brand's energy and style.

In the realm of public speaking and communication, cadence plays a pivotal role in conveying your message effectively. It influences the way your audience perceives your confidence, engagement, and respect for their time and attention. Unfortunately, many presenters fall into the habit of speaking too fast, often without realizing it, and this can have a detrimental impact on their personal brand.

The Rushed Cadence Dilemma

Speaking at a rapid pace is a common pitfall for many presenters, and it can be attributed to a range of factors. Nervousness is one of the primary culprits behind fast-paced speaking. When individuals are anxious about presenting, their adrenaline levels rise, leading to increased heart rate and faster speech. This heightened anxiety can be a result of various factors, including the fear of judgment, performance anxiety, or a lack of confidence in their content.

Unfortunately, many presenters try to mask their nervousness (from their audience, but also from themselves!) by pretending to be more confident than they actually are. They might adopt a brisk cadence in an attempt to appear in control and knowledgeable. However, this pretense often backfires, as it can come across as forced and insincere, eroding the trust and authenticity essential for personal branding.

Even more common among busy executives who are asked to speak at conferences and conventions is inadequate preparation. These presenters who have not thoroughly rehearsed their content tend to speak quickly. Perhaps it feels like they can to through their content as swiftly as possible, or it is simply the anxiety coming to the surface, or both. Regardless, this lack of preparation not only impacts the quality of the presentation but also reflects a disregard for the audience's experience.

Rapid speech can give the impression that you don't value your audience's time or comprehension. It signals a disregard for their ability to absorb and engage with your message. This lack of respect can undermine trust and diminish your personal brand's reputation. Your audience may struggle to follow your content, leading to confusion and frustration. Additionally, since attempting to project false confidence through speed can appear disingenuous, any perceived insincerity can erode the trust you aim to build with your audience.

There are some effective, and relatively simple things to improve your cadence. The first is to learn to recognize when you tend to speak quickly, especially in high-pressure situations. Self-awareness is the first step toward improvement. Once you have a good idea of your high-risk situations, thoroughly prepare and rehearse your presentations.

Yes. Really.

No one is so brilliant or naturally gifted as a presenter that they may be excused from doing the work. Familiarity with your content will boost your confidence and reduce anxiety, leading to more controlled cadence.

Of course, there are scenarios where that level of preparedness is not available, such as presidential addresses, or when we are asked to give an impromptu speech at a gathering. In both the prepared scenario and the unrehearsed variety, you can practice deep breathing techniques to manage nervousness and maintain a steady pace. Pausing to take a breath can slow your cadence and make your speech more manageable.

Regardless, as you are mastering your cadence, seek feedback from trusted peers, mentors, or coaches. They can help you identify when you're speaking too fast and provide guidance on how to improve. Also, don't be too proud to record your presentations and review them critically, much as an athlete would to improve their performance. This will help you pinpoint moments of rapid speech and work on pacing.

While rapid cadence is the most common challenge for leaders looking to build their brand, a slower pace may not be the answer. Certainly, it can indicate thoughtfulness, deliberation, and confidence. It's useful when discussing complex ideas, allowing your audience to digest information at a comfortable pace. However, speaking too slowly may come across as uncertainty, disinterest or lack of engagement.

The best cadence to strive for is the varied cadence. Like inflection, varying your cadence keeps your speech engaging. Mixing fast and slow pacing can emphasize key points, build anticipation, and maintain audience interest.

Body Language and Nonverbal Cues

In the world of personal branding, non-verbal cues and body language are as crucial as the spoken words themselves. Your gestures, facial expressions, and posture can enhance or detract from your message and personal brand. Let's explore some key types of body language and non-verbal cues for public speaking or video interviews that you can use to your advantage, as well as those that can hinder your impact:

Positive Non-Verbal Cues:

1. **Smiling:** A genuine smile can create an immediate connection with your audience. It conveys warmth, approachability, and enthusiasm. However, excessive smiling, especially in inappropriate moments, can appear insincere.

2. **Eye Contact:** Maintaining eye contact with your audience is a powerful way to establish trust and engagement. It signals that you are focused on them and interested in their response. Avoiding eye contact or staring at one individual for an extended period can make you seem disengaged or intimidating.

3. **Open Posture:** Standing tall with an open and relaxed posture communicates confidence and authenticity. It signals that you are approachable and receptive to feedback. Conversely, crossed arms can convey defensiveness or a closed-off attitude.

4. **Gestures for Emphasis:** Purposeful and natural hand gestures can enhance your message by emphasizing key points. They make your speech more dynamic and engaging. However, excessive or repetitive gestures can appear distracting or insincere.

Negative Non-Verbal Cues:

1. **Fidgeting:** Nervous habits like tapping your foot, playing with your hair, or constantly adjusting your clothing can distract your audience and signal anxiety or discomfort.

2. **Hands in Pockets:** Putting your hands in your pockets can convey a lack of confidence or professionalism. It can also make you appear disinterested or disconnected from your audience.

3. **Gripping the Podium:** Holding onto the podium for dear life can make you appear anxious or unprepared. It can also restrict your body's movements and limit your engagement with the audience.

4. **Pacing:** While some movement on stage is natural and can keep your audience engaged, excessive pacing can be distracting and make you seem restless or anxious.

5. **Stiff and Forced Gestures:** Using hand gestures is effective for emphasis, but when they feel forced or rehearsed, they can come across as inauthentic. It's essential to let your gestures flow naturally from your message.

The Impact of Emotional Tone on Personal Brand: Harnessing Your Emotional Range

Emotions are contagious. When you speak, your emotions become palpable to your audience. Whether it's excitement, passion, or empathy, your emotions create a connection that goes beyond words. Understanding how to harness and control these emotions is a crucial aspect of aligning your brand's voice with your authentic self.

Your emotional tone is capable of leaving a lasting impression on your audience. Just as a skilled singer uses their vocal range to convey a variety of emotions in a song, individuals must recognize and harness their emotional range to connect authentically with others. It's important to acknowledge that, like any human, we possess a wide vocabulary of emotions that are entirely appropriate depending on the context. The challenge lies in identifying this emotional range and utilizing it purposefully, much like a singer would use different notes and melodies to evoke different feelings in their audience.

Interestingly, many business leaders find themselves hesitant to display emotions, fearing it may compromise their professionalism or credibility. However, what they may not realize is that they are constantly projecting an emotional tone, whether they intend to or not. This subconscious emotional communication significantly influences their personal brand, taking direct control of their brand out of their hands. Rather than suppressing these emotions, successful leaders leverage them to their advantage. Emotions, when harnessed effectively, can convey authenticity, relatability, and a genuine connection with their audience.

For instance, consider a CEO addressing their team after a challenging quarter. She chose to express a blend of empathy for her team, and genuine concern for the serious situation they were facing. As a result, the CEO not only reinforced her identity as a compassionate leader but also cultivated an atmosphere accountability and responsibility to one another. Simultaneously, the CEO's optimism shone through, conveying a profound belief in the capabilities of her team to navigate difficulties.

This optimism carried with it a message of resilience and adaptability, indicating that the CEO was ready, and inviting her team, to pivot in the face of adversity. It's in that moment that the CEO encouraged her team to redouble their focus and effort in a fresh direction, highlighting that challenges are always present, and can be the catalyst for growth when met head-on. Her brand was powerful and present in the center of an emotional experience for everyone involved. Rather than pretend to be stoic, she tapped the emotions present for advancement.

On the other hand, consider a startup founder attempting to mask their emotions in front of potential investors. He was excited to present, and exceedingly nervous. He masked those emotions, since our founder's intention was to project an air of unflinching confidence and professionalism, which he believed was more modulated. Unfortunately, this attempt at emotional suppression unwittingly backfired. As he tried to hide his excitement and nervousness, he inadvertently created an emotional disconnect with the investors. The absence of visible excitement left the investors questioning whether the founder truly cared deeply about in his own vision.

Despite presenting lots of compelling data, when the investors probed for the founder's passion behind the business, they received responses couched in terms of market trends and analysis. This left the impression that the founder was disengaged and might not possess the resilience to weather obstacles that inevitably arise in the startup world.

Investors often seek entrepreneurs who not only have a sound business plan but also radiate unwavering passion and commitment. By concealing his genuine emotions, the startup founder missed a vital opportunity to establish a strong and authentic personal brand that resonated with the investors and left them confident in the founder's ability to navigate the challenges ahead.

In both scenarios, emotions are a powerful tool that contributes to a memorable and impactful personal brand. In the first it was intentional and authentic. In the second, it was unfortunately inauthentic and disastrous for the founder. When used purposefully and authentically, your emotional tone can help you connect with your audience on a deeper level, leaving a lasting and positive impression.

Crafting Your Personal Brand Message and Talking Points

Every leader and executive possess a unique set of values, beliefs, and principles that form the foundation of their personal brand. You found yours earlier. These values not only define who you are but also guide your decision-making and actions so they line up with your personal brand. What's more, identifying and articulating these core values allows you to translate them into a concise set of key talking points. A set of talking points is instrumental in shaping and reinforcing your personal brand across various platforms, from leadership roles to thought leadership, speeches, interviews, and even a book you might write.

Identifying and Engaging Your Target Audience as a Business Leader

As a business leader, whether you're an executive, founding CEO, or hold another influential role, understanding and connecting with your target audience is essential for shaping and advancing your personal brand. Importantly, this audience extends beyond a singular group; it comprises diverse segments, each with its unique needs and expectations. Identifying and engaging these distinct audience segments is key to your personal brand's growth and impact. Here's how to navigate this complex landscape:

Recognize the Multifaceted Audience: Start by recognizing that your audience is multifaceted. It includes your peers, who may share insights and opportunities, your internal team, whose motivation and alignment with your vision are vital, and those higher up the hierarchy, such as investors and boards, who have a say in your career trajectory. Additionally, your audience extends to thought leaders, industry peers, and the general public, all of whom can influence the trajectory of your personal brand.

Define Your Goals: Clearly define your goals in terms of personal brand growth—that's your vision and mission we uncovered earlier. Now, what steps and positions or opportunities are you striving for, and who can help you get there? Understanding your objectives will help you pinpoint the segments of your audience that are most relevant to your goals.

Seek Out Relevant Platforms: To connect with your target audience, you must be where they are. Attend industry conferences, join professional associations, and actively participate in online forums and social media communities relevant to your field. These platforms are fertile ground for engaging with peers, potential mentors, and industry influencers.

Tailor Your Message: Your audience segments have different needs and interests. Tailor your messaging to address these specific needs. For example, when it comes to your internal team, you might want to communicate your vision and values clearly to foster alignment. For investors or board members, you may choose to emphasize your strategic thinking and the value you bring to the organization (although, don't overlook the chance to bring those authentic emotions to bear as well!).

Build Meaningful Connections: Networking is more than just collecting business cards. It happens inside and outside an organization. It happens inside and outside of work as well. It's about cultivating meaningful relationships. Listen actively to your audience's concerns and perspectives. Offer support and insights where appropriate. Building genuine connections fosters mutual respect and opens doors to opportunities.

Provide Value: Your audience should see you as a source of value. Share your expertise through thought leadership articles, webinars, or speaking engagements. Contribute to discussions, solve problems, and offer insights. Demonstrating your value solidifies your reputation and reinforces your personal brand.

Be Willing to Adapt and Evolve: As your personal brand evolves, so too should your approach to engaging your audience. Stay attuned to industry trends, adapt your messaging, and seek opportunities to reinvent yourself. This adaptability ensures your continued relevance and growth within your target audience.

It can be easy to overlook that your target audience isn't static; it evolves as you progress in your career and personal brand journey. Continually reassess your goals and adjust your engagement strategies to remain aligned with your audience's evolving needs and expectations. As you keep these elements of your target audience in mind, you are now ready to develop those key talking points.

Develop Your Key Talking Points

Key talking points should be concise, memorable, and authentic expressions of your personal brand. They leverage your values, address the most prevalent needs of your audience, and are designed to move you towards your vision, as well as establishing a thought leadership position for you and your brand. Aim for three to five points that encapsulate your essence. Here are some examples:

1. **Integrity and Ethical Leadership:** "I believe in leading with unwavering integrity. Ethical leadership isn't just a choice; it's a commitment to doing what's right, even when it's challenging."

2. **Innovation and Change:** "My passion lies in driving innovation and embracing change. I'm convinced that by pushing boundaries and challenging the status quo, we can shape a brighter future."

3. **Empowerment and Mentorship:** "I'm committed to empowering individuals to reach their full potential. Mentorship isn't just about imparting knowledge; it's about unlocking the unique talents and capabilities within each person."

4. **Diversity and Inclusion:** "Diversity isn't just a buzzword; it's a cornerstone of progress. Inclusion is about ensuring that everyone's voice is heard, valued, and respected."

5. **Sustainability and Social Responsibility:** "Our responsibility extends beyond profit. I'm dedicated to fostering sustainability and social responsibility in every aspect of our organization, ensuring a better world for future generations."

These may not be your talking points. In fact, yours may vary wildly. Regardless what yours ultimatel are, talking points serve as the building blocks of your personal brand message. They can be adapted and woven into your leadership style, thought leadership content, speeches, interviews, and any other platform where you communicate your values and beliefs. Consistency in delivering these key points reinforces your personal brand, making it memorable and impactful for your audience. They also become the gateway to your thought leadership, which is the essence of personal branding.

CHAPTER 6

What's Your Story?

Every brand has a story. The catch is that your personal brand story really isn't about you! Yes, you have done all this work so far to identify your own unique and authentic values, vision, strengths and voice. But now we are going to take all those very important elements and use them to turn the spotlight on your ideal audience.

A compelling brand story resonates with your audience, keeps building that all-important trust, and lets them see themselves as an integral part of your personal brand—better for having engaged with you. While many confuse their brand's origin story with the brand story, we define brand story as the one which centers around your customers' experiences and aspirations. Whether you're a startup entrepreneur or an executive climbing the corporate ladder, your brand story is a key asset in your journey.

Building your personal brand story is somewhat akin to building your elevator pitch, although it is a bit more in-depth than the latter. It can be used in building your career advancement arc or growing your business. The principles are the same as are the steps in every great brand story. This chapter will be essentially a how-to build your brand story guide with two concurrent examples for a start-up sustainable clothing brand, Soul Sustainable Style, and a tech company executive, Mark, who ultimately has his eye on the CEO spot, and is using his story to help him get there.

Step 1: Understand Your Audience

Begin building your brand story by thoroughly understanding your target audience. There are countless resources, including on my website, Unstoppable-Leader.com under the tools tab, that will help you get crystal clear on your audience and how you can serve them and connect with them on an irresistible level. Your job is to identify what their needs, desires, pain points, and aspirations are. Your brand story should resonate with them on a personal level. Research and gather insights to create a customer persona that reflects your ideal audience. Then begin your brand story there. Let them see themselves reflected in it.

Soul Sustainable Styles:

There are a growing community of environmentally conscious consumers who want to make sustainable fashion choices without compromising on style or budget. We understand their desire to align their values with their clothing choices.

Mark:

I answer to a remarkable group of key stakeholders within my organization who are on the leading edge of this innovative technology, as well as being deeply connected with leading industry peers, and influencers setting the pace, who play a pivotal role in the growth and success of our company. I aim to build trust, credibility, and a strong network that recognizes my potential as a future leader of the company.

Step 2: Define Your Brand Promise

Now, assuming you have struck the right cord with your ideal audience and they feel like you and they are on the same page, it is time to tell them what, precisely, they can expect from you going forward. Remember, this must be 100% something you can deliver day-in and day-out, every single day. This is the crux of your values and vision. And it is nothing less than the foundation of your brand story and sets the stage for the rest of the narrative.

Soul Sustainable Styles:

We provide eco-conscious consumers with fashionable and affordable sustainable clothing options that allow them to express their style while making ethical choices.

Mark:

I am committed to consistently delivering exceptional results that meet or beat objectives, leading by example, and building and supporting a highly engaged team in my division that fosters growth, innovation, and collaborative success both in our organization and the broader industry.

Step 3: Create a Customer-Centric Narrative

At this point, the right audience is listening. Tell them more. Now, although your customers see themselves and their interests in your story so far, it is time to shift the focus from yourself or your business to your audience directly. Craft a narrative that highlights how your brand addresses their challenges and fulfills their aspirations. Use storytelling techniques to make your brand relatable and emotionally engaging.

Soul Sustainable Styles:

Our journey began with a passion for eco-conscious living. As we explored sustainable fashion options, we realized that there was a gap in the market. Many others shared our values, and that's when Soul Sustainable Styles was born.

Mark:

My career within our organization has been rich with opportunities to step into a thought leader position in this growing area of innovation, and the chance to recruit some of this generation's brightest and best minds, then instill them with a true growth mindset, so we can be ready to adapt and evolve at the pace we will certainly need to keep.

Step 4: Showcase Real Customer Experiences

That all sounds amazing, but why should anyone believe Soul Sustainable Style or Mark? Case studies and testimonials are the best route to social proof. Awards and industry recognition such as published articles and other press opportunities also work, but especially when paired with the former. Include real-life customer experiences and testimonials in your story and do not stoop to the auto-generated ones. If you are starting out, lean on testimonials to your character and approach if you must, but make them real, regardless. Share success stories, testimonials, and case studies that demonstrate the positive impact your brand has had on your customers' lives or businesses.

Soul Sustainable Styles:

Check out what one of our biggest fans, Emily, has to say about her experience with us: "I used to struggle to find eco-friendly clothing that I could afford. Soul Sustainable Styles changed that for me. They are great, on-trend and on-budget. Not only do I feel good about my purchases, but I also look great. I don't need to sacrifice style for living my values."

Mark:

I've had the privilege of collaborating with colleagues who have shared their experiences of how my guidance and innovative thinking have positively impacted projects we've taken on together, like Jean, who often says, "Mark has a talent for inspiring us to reach a level we didn't think was achievable before. I always want him on my team!"

Step 5: Highlight Your Unique Selling Points (USPs)

Once you have provided some track record and credibility to your story through these experiences, emphasize what sets you apart from the competition. Remember, your competition for a position in your existing organization, or another organization later, may be an unknown entity. This is also true in business competition, but in business you can Google, probe your networks and talk to prospective customers. Either way, this is where you are best served to lean on that unique combination of values and vision you have already established for yourself. That's your unassailable uniqueness and authenticity. And you can be supremely confident in those things in addition to your strengths and expertise in your chosen area. Explain how your brand's unique features and qualities directly benefit your customers.

Soul Sustainable Styles:

What sets us apart is our commitment to using eco-friendly materials, our transparent and ethical manufacturing practices, partnership with up-and-coming designers and our dedication to keeping our clothing accessible to everyone.

Mark:

What sets my approach apart is my unwavering commitment to continuous learning in a thriving team setting. It all comes down to always being willing to try, adapt, and learn even more. I will always be curious what we haven't tried, and where we can go next.

Step 6: Keep It Authentic

Authenticity is key. Your brand story should align with your brand's values and mission. Avoid over-promising or exaggerating; instead, focus on delivering on your brand promise. Underscoring your commitment to that can be lovingly at the expense of those who do not abide by the same levels of authenticity, which, sadly, there are too many of.

Soul Sustainable Styles:

We don't make exaggerated claims or greenwash our products. We're committed to delivering on our promise of affordable and sustainable fashion.

Mark:

We don't make exaggerated claims or greenwash our products. We're committed to delivering on our promise of affordable and sustainable fashion.

Where to Use Your Brand Story

Now that you've crafted your customer-centric brand story, let's explore where to use it for maximum impact:

1. **Website:** Your brand story should be prominently featured on your website's homepage. This is often the first place visitors look to learn about your brand.

2. **Social Media Profiles:** Share your brand story on social media platforms like LinkedIn, Facebook, or Instagram. It helps build a personal connection with your audience.

3. **Marketing Collateral:** Incorporate your brand story into your marketing materials, including brochures, flyers, and email campaigns.

4. **Pitch Presentations:** If you're a startup seeking investors or a young executive pitching a new idea, your brand story can captivate your audience and make your proposal more compelling.

5. **Networking Events and Conferences:** Use your brand story when introducing yourself to new contacts. It can make a lasting impression and initiate meaningful conversations.

6. **Content Marketing:** Weave elements of your brand story into your blog posts, videos, and other content. This can help build a consistent narrative across your digital presence.

7. **Networking:** You can share your brand story at networking events, emphasizing how your leadership journey aligns with your audience's aspirations.

8. **Job Interviews:** Incorporate elements of your brand story into job interviews, highlighting how your experiences and values resonate with the company's mission.

9. **Online Presence:** Feature your brand story on your personal website and LinkedIn profile to showcase your authenticity and leadership approach.

10. **Public Speaking:** Use your brand story during presentations and speaking engagements to establish credibility and inspire your audience.

11. **Mentorship:** Share your brand story with mentees to motivate and guide them in their own career journeys.

Your brand story evolves and grows right along with your brand. Keep it updated, and monitor the response it gets.

A final word of caution about your brand story – it doesn't work in a vacuum, and if you build it, post it on your website, and then expect it to do all the work for you, you are extremely likely to be disappointed. You need to be the one looking for platforms, stages, podcasts and media where you can tell your story over and over again as you are growing your brand.

CHAPTER 7

Thought Leadership: Elevating Your Influence

Thought leadership is a strategic approach in which an individual, organization, or business owner establishes themselves or their company as a recognized expert, authoritative voice, and innovator in a specific industry, field, or niche. Thought leaders are not merely knowledgeable about their domain but actively contribute valuable insights, original ideas, and solutions that shape and influence their category's direction.

However, the form thought leadership takes can be wildly variable and depends largely on what you want to accomplish with your personal brand. Thought leadership is such a grandiose and broad idea that very few individuals really know what it takes to achieve it, which is unfortunate, given thought leadership is the single most important attribute you must have to grow your personal brand effectively.

First, for business owners, thought leadership involves positioning themselves as industry experts to enhance their brand authority, reputation, and credibility.

Business owners who adopt a thought leadership strategy often focus on showcasing their company's expertise, differentiating their offerings, and attracting new customers or clients. Thought leadership can lead to increased brand visibility, customer loyalty, and revenue growth for the business.

Second, for individuals, thought leadership centers around establishing personal authority and expertise. Individuals pursuing thought leadership often aim to build a strong personal brand, gain recognition within their industry, and open up new career opportunities. Thought leaders may use various channels, such as publishing content, speaking engagements, and networking, to showcase their expertise and demonstrate value to their audience.

And third, thought leadership for managers and executives within organizations revolves around elevating the reputation and influence of the company. They act as brand ambassadors and subject matter experts for the organization, driving its industry positioning and thought leadership initiatives. Thought leaders in managerial or executive roles may engage in thought leadership through public speaking, industry collaborations, and thought-provoking content to advance their organization's objectives.

While the core principles of thought leadership remain consistent across these contexts, there are some differences in the strategies and goals based on the roles and objectives of business owners, individuals, and organizational managers/executives. Ultimately, thought leadership benefits each group by establishing expertise, fostering trust with stakeholders, and creating a positive impact on their respective industries.

Identifying Your Niche

Thought leadership is all about standing out. We know you are unique. You know what your focus and strategic direction are. You are even aware of your audience and their needs. Now it's time to synthesize all those things for optimum impact.

Finding a specific niche or area of expertise is crucial for anyone aiming to become a thought leader—and trust me, you want to aim for that if you want to make a meaningful impact. This specialization brings several vital advantages: It establishes your credibility as you cultivate profound knowledge and expertise in your chosen field, making you a recognized authority in a category you *really, truly can manageably cultivate such depth*. It also sets you apart from the crowd by providing a unique selling (even if you are the only thing you are promoting) proposition, differentiating you from generalists and competitors. In a world where information is abundant, standing out from the crowd is essential. Having a specialized niche helps you differentiate yourself from other generalists, making it easier for your audience to remember and recognize your expertise.

Moreover, by narrowing your focus, you can attract a more targeted audience interested in that specific topic. These individuals are more likely to engage with your content and see value in what you have to offer. Ultimately you will be able to address the unique challenges and pain points faced by your more narrowed audience in that area. This enables you to provide more insightful and relevant solutions, creating a deeper impact and fostering stronger connections with your tribe.

By focusing on a niche, you can create highly relevant and valuable thought leadership content that addresses the specific challenges, trends, and questions within your area of expertise. You become the go-to expert and advocate in that area, which can open up opportunities to collaborate and network with other professionals and thought leaders in that domain. These collaborations can further enhance your thought leadership and extend your reach, opening up opportunities for impactful contributions, allowing you to influence industry standards and drive innovation within your field.

It also bears mentioning, networking within your niche can lead to valuable collaborations, speaking engagements, and partnerships, further elevating your thought leadership status. In essence, narrowing your focus to a specific niche is a strategic move that enhances your credibility, enables you to create compelling content, and positions you as a recognized thought leader within your chosen domain.

It's also important to note that when you find yourself in a highly commoditized space or struggle to identify what makes you different, finding a specific niche or area of expertise to focus on for thought leadership can be challenging, but it is still possible. Here are some strategies to help you discover your unique angle:

Self-Assessment: Start by examining your own strengths, experiences, and passions even within what you have already uncovered. Identify the areas where you have excelled or gained valuable knowledge. Look for patterns and connections that might be unique or even innovative, such as connecting intuition and effective leadership. Reflect on what genuinely interests you and what you feel passionate about. Your authentic passion and enthusiasm for a topic can set you apart.

Audience Research: Conduct thorough research to understand your target audience's needs, pain points, and interests. Look for gaps or underserved areas within your industry or market. Consider reaching out to your existing network, conducting surveys, or participating in relevant online communities to gather insights.

Uniqueness in Your Story: Your personal and professional journey might hold unique experiences that others can learn from. Think about the challenges you've faced, the lessons you've learned, and the successes you've achieved. Sharing your story can differentiate you from others in a commoditized space.

Specialization within a Niche: Even in a crowded field, there may be narrower sub-niches that are not fully explored. Find opportunities to specialize within the broader area. For example, if you are in the fitness industry, instead of being a general fitness expert, you could focus on a specific type of workout or training for a particular audience (e.g., high performance athletes, seniors, pregnant women).

Innovative Approach: Consider bringing an innovative perspective to a well-established area. Think about how you can combine ideas from different fields, apply emerging technologies, or challenge conventional wisdom to provide fresh insights and solutions.

Solve a Specific Problem: Identify a pressing problem that your target audience faces and work on becoming the go-to resource for solving it. By positioning yourself as a problem solver, you establish credibility and authority.

Collaborate and Network: Engage with other experts and thought leaders in your industry. Collaborating with them can help you identify gaps and niches that others might have missed.

Test and Iterate: Don't be afraid to try different approaches and experiment with different topics. Test the waters with your content and see what resonates the most with your audience. Use analytics and feedback to guide your decision-making.

Focus on Your Audience's Journey: Instead of focusing solely on your expertise, consider the journey your audience is going through. Tailor your content to meet them at various stages of their journey, providing value and insights relevant to their specific needs.

Perseverance: Building thought leadership takes time and consistent effort. Be patient, stay committed to your chosen niche, and continually refine your messaging and positioning.

Remember, finding a specific niche doesn't happen overnight, especially in competitive or highly commoditized spaces. It requires introspection, research, and adaptability. Embrace the process of exploration and self-discovery, and over time, you will uncover your unique area of expertise that sets you apart as a thought leader.

Content Creation and Quality

Perhaps it is my writer's bias, but I strongly believe that the most valuable part of any personal brand is its content. I am not referring to content that is borrowed (or outright ripped off) from others. Nor do I mean content designed to dazzle and impress for the sake of creating a splash. I'm talking about real, meaningful, well thought out, clearly articulated content that moves you, your brand, your thought leadership, your business and even your industry forward. We need you. And you need great content.

Content can be intimidating to a lot of leaders. We know what we want to say, but we aren't quite sure how to say it. But that's putting the cart a bit before the horse. First let's look at what great content gets you.

The essential payoff for your content is to showcase your deep knowledge and expertise on specific subjects (you have that deep knowledge, right?). By consistently producing informative and insightful content, you build credibility among your audience, peers, and stakeholders, positioning themselves as go-to sources for reliable information. For the record, this content isn't even necessarily for your website, social media, podcasts or speeches. It can be in your networking circles, coffee break and water cooler conversations, or a chat with a fellow traveler on a plane. Much like the line in *Glengarry Glen Ross*, "ABC. Always Be Conversing." Oh. Wait. That's not what they said. But we will use it here. Practice your content in every situation, with fresh language, until it is a part of your DNA.

When thought leaders consistently provide valuable and accurate information, they earn the trust of their audience. Trust is a result of reliable and insightful content. People naturally follow and respect those they trust because trusted sources of content create value. This will mean that you will be invited to initiate discussions on emerging trends, challenges, and innovations within your industry. By creating thought-provoking content, you inevitably stimulate conversations and influence the direction of industry discourse.

No pressure!

The important thing to keep in mind is there really is no shortcut to great content. You can certainly begin building it as a practice—learning, adapting and evolving as you see what lands and what flops. Just keep n mind that great content is designed to go beyond self-promotion; it focuses on educating and inspiring the audience. To do that, you must educate yourself through immersion. Whether through articles, videos, webinars, or social media posts, your thought leadership will add value to your audience's careers and lives. To do that, you need to have done the work yourself, and discovered some powerful ideas worth sharing.

You will know when you have found your truly great content, because it inevitably sets you apart. In crowded markets, swimming in sameness and endless echo chambers of mediocrity, thought leadership sets individuals or organizations in a league of their own. At its core, thought leadership is built on showcasing unique perspectives and insights that stand out and create a niche. This is not for the faint of heart. But you won't be a thought leader by imitation. The best content challenges conventional thinking and encourage innovation.

To establish thought leadership through content effectively, it's essential to prioritize quality over quantity. Content should be well-researched, insightful, and tailored to the target audience's interests and needs. Additionally, you should engage with your audience at every opportunity, and actively participate in discussions to foster a genuine connection and build trust.

Taking A Stand to Stand Out

Taking a stance that is different from or counter to the common stance in your area of expertise can be a powerful way to stand out as a thought leader. It can help you challenge conventional wisdom, spark discussions, and offer a fresh perspective. However, it's essential to approach this strategy thoughtfully and with careful consideration.

Before advocating for a contrarian viewpoint, ensure that you have conducted in-depth research and analysis to support your stance. Strong evidence and data will make your argument more compelling. Although it can be tempting to drop a truth bomb of contradictory wisdom and just leave it there for impact, you really do need merit to back up your opinion. Clearly articulate why you believe the common stance in your field may be flawed or incomplete. Provide logical reasoning and draw on credible sources to back up your claims.

It is inevitable that sooner or later someone will take issue you're your stance, however uncontroversial you might believe it to be. The more of a thought leader you are, the more frequently this is bound to happen. Instead of resisting it, leverage it. Address the common counterarguments to your stance and explain why you think they may be misguided. Demonstrating that you've considered opposing views adds credibility to your position.

The most powerful part of this acknowledgement is the confidence and peer respect it demonstrates. When you deliver a contrarian viewpoint, maintain a respectful tone. Avoid being confrontational or dismissive of others' perspectives, as this can alienate your audience. Ultimately, remember, it is entirely okay to agree to disagree with a worthy adversary without getting down in the mud to slug it out to victory.

In fact, encouraging healthy debates and discussions around your content, inviting feedback and engaging with those who have differing opinions can enrich your thought leadership position—not harm it.

Establishing Expertise and Knowledge

Of course, in order to build that insightful content and identify a strong and innovative stance for yourself as a thought leader, it will be crucial that you make deepening your expertise and knowledge in a chosen niche a priority. That will become as much a part of who you are as the air you breathe, not a goal or a finish line where you can coast for the rest of your career enjoying the fruits of your thought leadership. Thought leadership is the prime stomping ground of individuals with growth mindset, and growth mindset lives to keep learning.

But it isn't a secret club we join either. There are endless ways you can dive into expertise and knowledge immersion. Here are just a few:

Online Courses and Tutorials: Enroll in online courses or tutorials specific to your niche. These are almost too abundant and accessible these days, and you will need to be careful about the source of information, nonetheless, platforms like Udemy, Coursera, LinkedIn Learning, and Skillshare offer a wide range of courses taught by experts in various fields. For instance, if you're in the field of data science, you could take a course on machine learning algorithms or data visualization.

Reading Specialized Books and Publications: Stay updated with the latest trends, research, and developments in your niche by reading books, whitepapers, research papers, and industry publications. For instance, if you're interested in entrepreneurship, you might read books like *The Lean Startup* by Eric Ries or *Zero to One* by Peter Thiel.

Participate in Webinars and Webcasts: Many organizations and experts host webinars or webcasts on niche-specific topics. These events often feature industry leaders sharing insights and best practices. Look for webinars related to your niche and participate actively by asking questions and engaging with the speakers.

Create Content and Share Knowledge: Establish yourself as an authority in your niche by creating and sharing valuable content. You can start a blog, write articles, a book or create videos on topics relevant to your field. This not only helps deepen your understanding but also allows you to contribute to the community and build your reputation.

Collaborate with Peers and Mentors: Networking with peers and mentors in your niche can provide invaluable insights and support. Don't be afraid to Engage in discussions with them, seek advice, and learn from their experiences. Professional platforms like LinkedIn can be a great place to connect with industry experts.

Attend Niche-Specific Meetups: Search for local or online meetups focused on your niche. These gatherings provide opportunities to interact with like-minded individuals, discuss current challenges, and share knowledge. Websites like Meetup.com often list such events.

Volunteer or Freelance in Your Niche: Practical experience is essential for deepening expertise. Consider volunteering for projects or freelancing in your niche to apply your knowledge and gain hands-on experience. For example, if you are in the field of graphic design, you might volunteer to design promotional materials for a non-profit organization.

Cross-Training in Related Disciplines: Sometimes, expertise in one field can be enhanced by understanding related disciplines. If your niche is marketing, for example, learning about consumer psychology or UX design could complement your skills.

Conduct Research and Case Studies: Undertake independent research and case studies related to your niche. This helps you gain a deeper understanding of the subject matter and potentially uncover new insights.

Engage in Online Forums and Communities: Join online forums and communities dedicated to your niche. Actively participate in discussions, answer questions, and seek feedback. Platforms like Reddit, Stack Exchange, and Quora can be great resources for this purpose.

Combining some or even all of these strategies will help you become a recognized authority in your chosen niche and open up new opportunities for personal and professional growth.

Your Thought Leadership In Action

If you are a busy CEO or executive, creating a thought leadership platform for yourself can feel almost overwhelming. It is true that it is a nuanced process requiring careful planning and efficient time management. Essentially, you need a strategy, and depending on where you are in the process, and where you want your thought leadership to take you, you need a strategy now. A thought leader's strategy isn't that different than a marketing strategy for any business, yet it seems there is no branding or marketing effort more challenging than the one you do for yourself.

Although you may find some of the following steps to be a bit of a no-brainer, before you write them off as too pedantic, ask yourself, are you really doing them? Or is your effort at thought leadership a bit more scattershot than you care to admit? You might get a TED talk, or have more than one bestseller under your belt – but how are you leveraging those in your overall strategy? How are you squeezing the most juice out of all that effort you put into them? So here is a step-by-step guide (and the steps are in order for a reason) on how to create a thought leadership strategy while managing your already substantial existing responsibilities—read it. Be honest about what you are really doing, and where you know you need to revise and adapt:

1. **Set Clear Goals:** Define specific and measurable goals for your thought leadership efforts. Determine what you want to achieve, whether it's brand awareness, industry recognition, lead generation, or preparing for your next career move.

2. **Identify Your Unique Angle:** This is that combination of your values, vision, your authentic self, who you can serve and all that great content you have built.

3. **Delegate and Outsource:** Recognize that you can't do everything yourself. Delegate tasks to your team or consider outsourcing aspects of your thought leadership strategy such as content creation, social media management, or website development.

4. **Focus on Content Creation:** Create valuable content that showcases your expertise. This can include articles, blog posts, whitepapers, videos, and more. Consider starting with a book, as it can serve as a cornerstone piece of thought leadership.

5. **Build a Content Calendar:** Plan your content in advance and create a content calendar. Allocate specific times for content creation and stick to your schedule. Consistency is key in building an audience. If you are

already speaking or have written a book and skipped this step, you have jumped ahead of the process.

6. **Tap Existing Resources:** Utilize your existing knowledge and resources. Repurpose presentations, reports, or experiences into public-facing content. This can save time and leverages your existing hard-won credibility.

7. **Leverage Social Media Strategically:** Choose a few key social media platforms where your target audience is active. Share your content, engage with your audience, and establish yourself as an authority in your niche. You can certainly schedule posts in advance to save time, but this effort is critical in today's landscape, and it takes strategy, commitment and spot-on messaging. If you don't have the time or track record of success in this arena, find someone who does, and hire them.

8. **Garner Professional Speaking Engagements:** Search out and select speaking opportunities that align with your goals and expertise. I was once asked, as an inexperienced speaker, to give a leadership presentation to a kennel club. They historically had had veterinarians and dog trainers to speak and wanted "something different." Alarm bells should have gone off. While it wasn't horrible, neither the client nor myself were thrilled with the outcome. It simply was not a good fit. Rather than accepting every invitation, focus on high-impact events that reach your target audience.

9. **Use Networking and Collaboration:** Collaborate with other thought leaders, influencers, and industry experts. Guest post on their platforms or participate in joint webinars, podcasts, or events to expand your reach. No matter how high you have risen, there are always fantastic opportunities to grow your audience this way.

10. **Build a Personal Brand Website:** Create a professional website that serves as a hub for your thought leadership content. Include a bio, portfolio, blog, and contact information. Consider hiring a web developer to ensure your site is an impeccable representation of your brand, and does not unwittingly undermine your efforts by appearing unprofessional or amateurish.

11. **Get a Thought Leadership Team:** If feasible, consider hiring or appointing a thought leadership team to manage aspects of your strategy. This team could include a content manager, social media manager, speaker agent, book publisher, for example.

12. **Measure and Adapt:** Because you paused to reflect on your goals, you have an idea of what success ought to look like, and so you are able to continuously monitor the performance of your thought leadership efforts. Analyze metrics like website traffic, social media engagement, and lead generation. Adjust your strategy based on what works best.

13. **Use Your Time Wisely:** Most of the clients I work with to build their thought leadership are extraordinarily busy. But thought leadership efforts take a great deal of additional time, and there are no shortcuts. You will need to plan on dedicating specific blocks of time to your thought leadership efforts. This might involve early mornings, evenings, or weekends. Protect these time slots as you would any other business commitment. It's worth it.

14. **Seek Professional Help:** That leads us to the reason people like myself exist. Although building your thought leadership brand effort takes time, much of which only you can do, a professional can minimize your heavy lifting, and help you avoid costly delays and missteps. Once you reach a certain point, consult with a personal branding agency specializing in thought leadership. They can provide guidance and support tailored to your goals.

Is Thought Leadership Personal Branding?

There are distinctive differences between personal branding and thought leadership. The key difference is that thought leadership is a very specific type of personal brand, and no, you do not need to be a thought leader in order to have a distinctive personal brand. Both terms are tossed around today quite freely, so let's clear it up here.

Personal branding, as we have already said, revolves around shaping and managing your public image, values, and how others perceive you. It aims to establish a consistent and favorable identity, often for career advancement, reputation management, or building trust with a broad or specific audience. It encompasses elements like personal stories, values, mission, voice, style, and public-facing presence. It can manifest through social media, personal websites, and other self-presentation channels. You might use it to build a business, and you might use it to advance your career. The idea here is to be very intentional about how you show up as thoroughly and authentically yourself, playing to your strengths.

Thought leadership, on the other hand, focuses on becoming a recognized expert or authority in a particular field or industry. It involves offering unique insights, expertise, and solutions to industry-specific challenges, with the goal of influencing and inspiring others in that niche. Candidly, it takes even more intentional, committed effort than building your personal brand.

Thought leadership is characterized by deep industry knowledge, innovative thinking, and the ability to provide solutions to complex problems. It primarily targets a niche or industry-specific audience and is often conveyed through industry publications, speaking engagements, and specialized conferences.

While personal branding and thought leadership are distinct concepts, they can complement each other. Personal branding can enhance your thought leadership efforts by creating a positive and consistent image, while thought leadership showcases your expertise and authority in a specific area. Together, they can help you build a strong professional identity and make a significant impact.

CHAPTER 8

Made You Look

Like it or not, we are judged based on how we look. It is a part of the human experience. In a world where first impressions are formed in seconds and unconscious biases are omnipresent, building your personal brand means proactively managing your visual identity and online presence. By doing so, you can ensure that your true abilities and character shine through, ultimately making a positive impression from the start.

Human nature tends to lead us to judge others based on appearances because it's an innate survival mechanism. Throughout our evolutionary history, quick judgments about people and situations helped us assess potential threats and make split-second decisions. While this trait can be advantageous in certain situations, it can also lead to biases and snap judgments that may not accurately reflect a person's true brand essence.

First impressions are formed astonishingly fast, often within the first 7 seconds of encountering someone or something new. This initial impression is heavily influenced by appearance, body language, and other visual cues. Unfortunately, these snap judgments can be challenging to overcome because they are deeply ingrained in our subconscious.

This tendency to judge quickly extends to the digital realm as well. On the internet, it takes just 3 seconds for a visitor to decide whether to stay on a website based on its appearance and usability. This phenomenon, known as "bounce rate," highlights the importance of a visually appealing and user-friendly website.

Human bias, both conscious and unconscious, plays a significant role in these rapid judgments. In my book, *Inside Out Smart*, I discuss how there are seven common biases that can have a serious impact on our ability to make effective decisions, especially when the pressure is on. Preconceived notions, stereotypes, and personal experiences can all influence how we perceive others and the content we encounter every day in growing volumes. These biases help us sort the information quickly, albeit often incorrectly, and can be difficult to counteract, even when confronted with clarifying information. This makes it almost impossible to have a branding "do over" if your visual brand is off-point or off-putting to your core audience.

So, rather than try to fight human nature, we branders have devised a way to help you identify the visual components that really do project your authentic brand, and then leverage them. Far from being inauthentic, it actually means your visual presence can do a lot of the heavy lifting in communicating your brand and what you stand for before you even enter the actual or metaphorical room.

The Five Brand Personalities

Every brand, personal or business, has a personality, just like we do as individuals. And like individuals, they can be cultivated, and enhanced. What's more, we cannot visually present ourselves with one personality when we really identify with another one with much success. It just does not resonate with other people who can sense its falseness, even if they aren't sure why.

Therefore, it should be no surprise that brand personalities play a pivotal role in establishing emotional connections, differentiation, and loyalty. They don't show up strictly on a visual level, since they also are reflected in our values, our mission and our voice. However, the visual component of our brand personality is often the first contact we make, and therefore, possibly the most important aspect of our personal brand.

Brand personalities help you to connect with your target audience on an emotional level and convey your values and characteristics effectively. Here are a list of the five brand personalities, the descriptive words most often identified with each one, and three examples of consumer brands that are generally categorized with each personality. You can perhaps draw inspiration from these brand personalities as you are developing your personal brand to create a consistent and relatable image.

The Sophisticated Brand

Descriptive Words: Elegant, refined, upscale, luxurious, classic
Consumer Brand Examples:
- **Chanel:** Known for its timeless and elegant fashion and accessories.
- **Rolex:** A luxury watch brand associated with sophistication and prestige.
- **Mercedes-Benz:** A high-end automobile manufacturer synonymous with sophistication and style.

The Sincere Brand

Descriptive Words: Authentic, trustworthy, genuine, friendly, down-to-earth
Consumer Brand Examples:
- **Dove:** Promotes authenticity and body positivity through its beauty and personal care products.
- **Whole Foods:** Emphasizes fresh and wholesome ingredients, projecting sincerity in its approach to food.
- **TOMS:** Known for its commitment to social responsibility, TOMS shoes exude sincerity through its "One for One" giving model.

Competent

Descriptive Words: Professional, reliable, knowledgeable, capable, confident
Consumer Brand Examples:

- **Home Depot:** A home improvement and renovation retailer that provides know-how and expertise in-store and contractors to execute when the consumer prefers vendor support.
- **McKinsey & Company:** A management consulting firm renowned for its competence in providing business solutions.
- **Google:** The dominant source for online search and information about almost any topic in an instant globally.

The Excitement Brand

Descriptive Words: Energetic, dynamic, fun, bold, adventurous
Consumer Brand Examples:
- **Red Bull:** The energy drink that associates itself with excitement and adventure.
- **Nike:** Known for its "Just Do It" slogan, promoting an active and adventurous lifestyle.
- **GoPro:** The action camera company that captures and shares thrilling experiences.

The Rugged Brand

Descriptive Words: Tough, durable, outdoorsy, practical, no-nonsense
Consumer Brand Examples:
- **The North Face:** A brand specializing in outdoor apparel and gear for rugged adventures.
- **Jeep:** Known for its rugged and off-road vehicles designed for durability.
- **Caterpillar:** A manufacturer of construction and industrial equipment, projecting ruggedness and strength.

While a brand typically has one dominant personality, it can exhibit elements of other personalities as well. This concept is known as a "hybrid brand personality." The dominant personality is the one that aligns most closely with the brand's core values and resonates most strongly with its target audience.

Brands that exhibit elements of multiple personalities (no, that doesn't mean they have a multiple personality disorder!), should begin by identifying and maintaining a dominant personality that aligns with their core values and target audience to create a cohesive and memorable brand identity.

For example, a brand that primarily represents a "Sincere" personality but occasionally incorporates elements of "Excitement" to appeal to a younger audience may be considered a hybrid. However, the "Sincere" personality remains the dominant trait.

It's essential for brands to maintain consistency in their dominant personality because this is what consumers come to associate with the brand. Inconsistencies in branding can confuse consumers and dilute the brand's impact. Therefore, while flexibility is valuable, it should not compromise the clarity and consistency of the brand's identity.

While the brand personalities apply to every aspect of your brand – your voice, your story, your ideal audience and your values – they are most prominent in the visual and experiential aspect of your brand. They reflect your story, values and voice, but they are projected in how you look.

If you are not sure about your brand personality, or are waffling between two or three, take the brand personality assessment quiz at tinyurl.com/5brandpersonalities.

The Color of You

First of all, there is no color that is off limits for your brand. Everyone has a yellow they can wear. It just depends on the hue and intensity, which might be a lemon yellow, canary yellow, mustard, chartreuse, or cream. What's more, no one is ever going to wear just one color. You may favor a particular color or shade, but our personalities are never monochromatic, and therefore, neither are our brands.

When I am helping a business brand determine what colors to use, we look at the owner or leadership team's favorite colors, and we do this in concert with the business' values. Almost always the colors they are personally and emotionally drawn to line up perfectly with their values and their brand personality.

Conversely, when they start looking at what other businesses in their category are using and either try to match those brands' colors, or be the standout by being thoroughly different, they lose their authenticity immediately. Choose your colors based on who you are, not what everyone around you is doing, or not doing.

Color theory is based in psychology. It is foundational to effective marketing and branding's subliminal appeal. Designers and marketers can spend years studying and applying them. However, you don't need to become an expert in color theory to choose the most effective colors of your brand. A high-level understanding should suffice. The best advice I can give is to trust your gut, and be willing to explore various shades, hues and combinations of color until you land on what resonates both who you are, and with your audience.

For our purposes, here is a list of the main colors of the color theory wheel, the emotions each evokes, what brand personalities commonly use each, and how combining them with other colors can add depth to what they communicate in isolation. I will share some broad pairings with neutrals and with tertiary colors, but keep in mind, they are far from all-inclusive:

Red:
- **Evokes:** Passionate, Energetic, Love, Bold, Dynamic, Exciting
- **Brand Personalities:** Excitement (e.g., Coca-Cola), Sincere (e.g., Hallmark), Competent (e.g., Target)
- **Pairings:** Red pairs well with gray for a balanced and sophisticated look. It also creates a striking contrast with black or white. When red is combined with burgundy or maroon adds depth and intensity to your brand.

Blue:
- **Evokes:** Trustworthy, Calm, Stable, Serene, Professional, Reliable
- **Brand Personalities:** Competent (e.g., IBM), Sincere (e.g., American Express), Rugged (e.g., Ford)
- **Pairings:** Blue complements beige or light gray for a calming and professional appearance. Navy blue pairs well with white for a timeless look. Teal or aqua shades of blue bring vibrancy and freshness to your color scheme.

Yellow:
- **Evokes:** Optimistic, Happy, Creative, Playful, Warm, Sunny
- **Brand Personalities:** Excitement (e.g., McDonald's), Sincere (e.g., IKEA), Rugged (e.g., CAT)

- **Pairings:** Yellow works harmoniously with gray or white for a cheerful and clean aesthetic. It can also be balanced with beige. Pairing yellow with mustard or ochre can create warmth and genuineness in your color palette.

Green:

- **Evokes:** Growth, Harmonious, Natural, Refreshing, Calming, Balanced
- **Brand Personalities:** Sincere (e.g., Whole Foods), Competent (e.g., John Deere), Rugged (e.g., The North Face)
- **Pairings:** Green combines beautifully with beige or soft gray for a natural and calming effect. Darker greens work well with black for a more dramatic look. Olive green paired with earthy brown tones adds a sense of groundedness and earthiness.

Purple:

- **Evokes:** Luxurious, Creative, Regal, Mysterious, Elegant, Enigmatic
- **Brand Personalities:** Sophisticated (e.g., Cadbury), Excitement (e.g., Yahoo!), Sincere (e.g., Hallmark)
- **Pairings:** Purple can be paired with gray or white for an elegant and modern appearance. Deep purples can be striking with black. Combining purple with lavender or lilac hues adds a soft and dreamy quality to your palette.

Orange:

- **Evokes:** Energetic, Enthusiastic, Playful, Vibrant, Friendly, Invigorating
- **Brand Personalities:** Excitement (e.g., Fanta), Sincere (e.g., Home Depot), Rugged (e.g., Harley-Davidson)
- **Pairings:** Orange contrasts nicely with gray or beige, creating a vibrant and balanced combination. It also pops against black or white, while terracotta or rust shades of orange lend a calming and even naturalistic feel to your brand.

Black:

- **Evokes:** Sophisticated, Powerful, Elegant, Timeless, Edgy, Formal
- **Brand Personalities:** Sophisticated (e.g., Chanel), Competent (e.g., Apple), Excitement (e.g., Nike)

- **Pairings:** Black can be paired with gray or white for a timeless and minimalist look. Adding beige softens the contrast. When black is combined with any tertiary color the effect is one of even stronger elegance, trustworthiness, and confidence.

White:
- **Evokes:** Pure, Clean, Simple, Minimalist, Fresh, Open
- **Brand Personalities:** Sincere (e.g., Dove), Sophisticated (e.g., Apple), Competent (e.g., IBM)
- **Pairings:** White pairs seamlessly with beige, creating a fresh and airy atmosphere. It also contrasts elegantly with black or gray. Adding white and a tertiary color creates an enhanced mood of openness, peace and simplicity.

Gray:
- **Evokes:** Neutral, Balanced, Versatile, Modern, Professional, Calm
- **Brand Personalities:** Sophisticated (e.g., Mercedes-Benz), Competent (e.g., LinkedIn), Sincere (e.g., Toyota)

Beige:
- **Evokes:** Subtle, Timeless, Warm, Earthy, Conservative, Comforting
- **Brand Personalities:** Sincere (e.g., PayPal), Competent (e.g., General Electric), Sophisticated (e.g., Ralph Lauren)

Brown/Tan:
- **Evokes:** Earthy, Warm, Reliable, Natural, Timeless, Comforting
- **Brand Personalities:** Rugged (e.g., Timberland), Sincere (e.g., UPS), Sophisticated (e.g., Hershey's)

Combining colors effectively with neutrals and tertiary colors allows for more nuanced and multifaceted communication in personal style and branding. Remember that different hues within each color category can evoke different emotions. For instance, a bright emerald green conveys a sense of vitality and growth, while an olive green suggests earthiness and stability. When selecting colors for your personal style or brand, consider the specific emotions and associations you want to convey, and experiment with various combinations to create a visually appealing and emotionally resonant palette.

Using Personal Style to Project Your Brand

Your personal style serves as the foundation of your visual identity, whether you are building your brand to advance your career or your business. A well-crafted visual identity is instrumental in building a strong personal brand. It should be carefully aligned with your chosen brand personality, whether it's Sophisticated, Sincere, Competent, Excitement, or Rugged.

Your attire, environment, video chat platform background, website, slide template, business card, social media posts, photography and every other visual aspect of your brand that the world can see are critical channels for communicating—or miscommunicating—what your real brand personality is. If you capture your brand personality effectively, your ideal audience will be attracted to you. If not, a non-ideal audience will be, and then they will feel misled over time when they realize that false image is not who you really are.

Your brand's visual elements should work harmoniously to convey your brand's values, expertise, and unique personality. By integrating them effectively across all visual the touchpoints we listed above using fonts, brand colors, photos or illustrations that communicate your brand personality, you'll create a memorable and compelling personal brand that opens doors to new opportunities—the right opportunities you are seeking to cultivate.

How that looks is often the realm of a personal stylist, a graphic designer, or other professional. You may want to hire one or more of these individuals to assist you. However, what follows is the high-level way your brand might begin to take visual form.

Remember, again, there are no hard and fast rules about style, color or fonts. How you assemble it together is where your brand message is ultimately communicated. For example, given how pink can be seen as inherently feminine (think Barbie, the movie) but can also evoke a retro vibe, and even be an excitement brand if combined with black and bold, strong fonts, your awareness of what each element means and how to assemble them to be a definitive expression of who you are is what matters. In the end, your combination will be uniquely and entirely you alone.

Sophisticated Brand Expressed

A sophisticated brand personality exudes elegance and refinement:

- **Personal Style:** Opt for classic, timeless clothing choices with clean lines and muted colors.
- **Font Choices:** Select elegant, serif fonts like Times New Roman or Baskerville.
- **Colors:** Use black, deep blues, and rich burgundy for a sense of sophistication and luxury.

Sincere

A sincere brand personality focuses on authenticity and trustworthiness:

- **Personal Style:** Choose approachable and down-to-earth attire, avoiding overly formal or flashy clothing.
- **Font Choices:** Consider simple, sans-serif fonts like Futura or Helvetica for a clean and honest look.
- **Colors:** Earthy tones, warm blues, and gentle greens convey sincerity and reliability.

Competent

A competent brand personality emphasizes professionalism and expertise:

- **Personal Style:** Look for tailored, well-fitted clothing that communicates competence and attention to detail.
- **Font Choices:** Use strong, clean, and modern sans-serif fonts like Century Gothic or Avenir.
- **Colors:** Stick to bold, confident colors like navy blue, deep red, and charcoal gray.

Excitement

An excitement brand personality is dynamic and energetic:

- **Personal Style:** Embrace bold and vibrant clothing choices that reflect enthusiasm and energy.

- **Font Choices:** Go for playful or energetic fonts like a handwritten style font or Impact.
- **Colors:** Bright and energetic colors like red, orange, and yellow invoke excitement and positivity.

Rugged

A rugged brand personality signifies toughness and durability:

- **Personal Style:** Choose rugged and practical clothing, such as denim and workwear-inspired outfits.
- **Font Choices:** Seek out sturdy and rustic fonts like Courier or Rockwell.
- **Colors:** Earthy tones like browns, greens, and rustic reds convey ruggedness and reliability.

Obviously, this only scratches the surface of what is possible. For example, given how many fonts there are—in 2015 it was estimated there were well over 300,000, and that number is growing at a rapid clip every year—it would be impossible to list all that is available. I have not (for my designerly friends reading this) chosen the most trend-forward fonts, since not only do those trends come and go, but for most of us trying to build a brand, we need those which are readily available to pretty much anyone and everyone with little effort. There are countless resources to explore for clothing, fonts and all your style "accessories" – so play, explore, and have fun. Just use what I am sharing as a starting point.

Being Seen

Like the colors, fonts and personal style your brand lands on, there is an equally vast array of areas where you can be visible. Some are necessary, such as a *professional* headshot, while others depend on what you are trying to accomplish for yourself and your brand, like particular social media platforms.

For each area of visibility, rather than trying to become an expert in the technology and methodology, become the best expert possible for your brand personality. Then hire an expert in the tech and form. It works best that way. You make sure they promote your brand (which must be *your* expertise) using their expertise in a particular format. Together you will be far more successful. Here are some of the areas—again, not remotely all of those possible—for you to consider growing your visibility with. You don't need to know about lighting, sound, promotion, algorithms, frequency of content, or anything other than what you sound like, look like, your story and your talking points. Goodness knows that is a lot all by itself!

Professional Headshots

A well-crafted *professional* headshot plays a pivotal role in your visual identity. This is a non-negotiable. Seriously. You cannot do what a pro can do. I am amazed at the number of executives, business owners, and leaders who either do not have a professional headshot (and no, paying your nephew, the photography student, to take a photo of you in the back yard does not count!) or have a headshot so outdated that it barely resembles you—and sure, we all wish we looked like we did at 24, but you look gorgeous just as you are, and a lot more confident, actually. So if you don't have one of these, get one now! And if yours is not a good representation of your personal brand, then get one that is, stat!

Professional means it is well lit, captures your presence and your brand, is in a neutral or polished setting, and is current to who you are today, and what you look like in the present.

- **Sophisticated:** Capture headshots with a luxe or rich setting. The polish and professionalism will exude the right tone of elegance.
- **Sincere:** Maintain a warm and approachable smile in your headshot. Keep the setting simple and natural.
- **Competent:** Choose a headshot that exudes confidence and professionalism. Setting yourself in the context of your work is a plus here.
- **Excitement:** Use dynamic and energetic poses and facial expressions.
- **Rugged:** Opt for bold settings and take a stance of strength.

Brand Photos and Imagery

Visual storytelling through brand photos and imagery should align with your brand personality. Most business owners will look at this and think about photos and imagery applied to their website, social media, or printed materials. But it goes beyond that. Think about your presentation to the management conference. Your Facebook or Instagram feeds. What does your blog imagery look like? And let's not forget your speaker one sheet or your book cover!

In a perfect world your brand imagery will lean only lightly on stock photos or illustrations, but if you must use stock visuals, make sure they feature your brand colors and personality, and are as representative of your ideal client as possible.

- **Sophisticated:** Showcase upscale venues, luxury products, and refined settings.
- **Sincere:** Share behind-the-scenes glimpses of your authentic self and your journey.
- **Competent:** Highlight professional settings, awards, and accomplishments.
- **Excitement:** Use action shots, vibrant colors, and enthusiastic expressions.
- **Rugged:** Feature rugged, natural landscapes and authentic, unfiltered moments.

Video Style

Video is the highest ranked content on social media and by search engines like Google, which owns YouTube. But that doesn't mean just any video will do. If you are a competent brand, and I see you dancing around in a TikTok video then you had better be a dancer or dance instructor. "Hey! Look at me!" does nothing for your brand if what I see is out of alignment with what you are all about.

Bad lighting, subpar audio, poor or missing captions, lack of editing, and other amateur oversights undermine your visible branding. They undermine your brand. Period. So, either use video to grow your brand visibility or opt out of this media altogether. That goes for Instagram Reels, YouTube vlogs, Facebook Lives, as well as podcasts with video components, and corporate videos.

Your video content style should be consistent with your brand personality:

- **Sophisticated:** Use polished, cinematic videography and articulate speech.
- **Sincere:** Emphasize authenticity and personal stories in your videos.
- **Competent:** Employ professional graphics, clear explanations, and a knowledgeable tone.
- **Excitement:** Incorporate energetic visuals, music, and a dynamic on-screen presence.
- **Rugged:** Shoot videos in natural, unpolished settings and use straightforward, no-nonsense language.

Logo and Website

Whether you are looking to advance your business or career, you may need a website. For the professional the website may be for their book, there speaking, or for a community they have built. Businesses will eventually need to look at both a logo *and* a website. Notice, however, that I said *eventually*. Too many brands jump the rails and create a website and logo—often investing thousands of dollars to do so, before they have honed in on their personal brand. The results might look professional, but rarely are they a good representation of what makes the business or individual unique and compelling to their audience.

So do your brand work first. Then, and only then, lean into creating the logo or website that tells your story effectively. Remember also that your website is not about you. It is about your audience. It lets them feel seen, understood and connected to a solution they crave. Take them on a clearly identified and mapped out journey of connection and trust-building with you. And of course, do it all in your brand personality's style:

- **Sophisticated:** A minimalistic, elegant logo and a sleek, informative website. Showcase your own success, the company you keep, and your high-quality products and services.
- **Sincere:** A warm, approachable logo and a content-rich, personable website. Include lots of testimonials and practical advice.

- **Competent:** A strong, professional logo and an organized, informative website. Case studies, credentials, recognition and industry involvement help promote your brand.
- **Excitement:** A lively, dynamic logo and an engaging, interactive website. You are innovative and leading edge, on-trend and a little bit daring. A blog or training that helps your audience gain access to your techniques and approach is a great way to go. Bonus points if you create your own app!
- **Rugged:** A rugged, straightforward logo and a no-frills, functional website. Your site is not about the verbal content. It is about the experience and the results. For you, a picture (or a video) is worth a thousand words. Show your audience, don't tell them.

Social Media

Social media undeniably plays a pivotal role in elevating a personal brand's visibility in today's digital age. I would be remiss in not listing it under the visual and visible aspects of your brand. However, it can be a double-edged sword. The vast and diverse landscape of social platforms can be noisy and overwhelming, often leaving individuals confused about where to start and how to stand out. Each platform caters to distinct demographics and behaviors, making it crucial for personal brand builders to choose wisely and align their content with their target audience. Otherwise, it is not only overwhelming, it takes every minute of your day, giving little back in return.

I will not even attempt to teach you anything about a particular platform or how to approach any of them. There are already countless books and experts offering guidance on mastering the algorithms and technologies of various social media platforms, should you prefer to add that to your expertise arsenal. At the same time there's a foundational principle that often gets overlooked: every post, tweet, or share is an opportunity to build and reinforce one's personal brand, both visually and in terms of content. It's not about mimicking the latest trends or emulating what everyone else is doing. Instead, it's about staying true to your unique identity and values while crafting content that resonates with your audience.

In the midst of the social media noise, authenticity and consistency become your most potent allies. Your personal brand should shine through in every piece of content you share. Whether it's the colors, fonts, or imagery you use, they should all reflect your brand's personality and story. Remember, the most impactful posts are those that engage, educate, or inspire your audience while staying aligned with your brand's core message. So, while mastering the technical aspects of social media can be an asset, never underestimate the power of genuine, visually compelling, and brand-aligned content to make a lasting impact.

CHAPTER 9

The Measure of Success

Too many of us—present company included—can become overly enamored with the creative and emotionally evocative aspects of our personal brand, and overlook the fact that it also needs to generate results. Otherwise, it is just a hobby.

But how do we measure whether our personal brand work is creating the impact we desire? How long should it take to see the results? There is no one-size-fits-all answer. The timeline for seeing measurable results from personal branding efforts can vary widely based on several factors, including your starting point, the industry or niche you're in, the consistency of your efforts, and the platforms you use. Here are some considerations:

Starting Point: If you're starting with a strong existing network, relevant skills, or a unique value proposition, you may see results more quickly. Conversely, if you're building your brand from scratch, it might take longer to gain traction.

Consistency: Consistency is key in personal branding. Regularly posting valuable content, networking, and engaging with your audience can accelerate your results. Building trust and recognition often takes time, so a sustained effort is crucial.

Platform Choice: The platform you choose for personal branding can impact the timeline. For example, some social media platforms may yield quicker results in terms of engagement, while long-term content efforts like blogging or podcasting may take longer to gain a significant following.

Industry or Niche: The competitiveness of your industry or niche can also affect the timeline. In highly competitive fields, it may take longer to stand out and gain recognition.

Content Quality: High-quality, valuable content tends to attract an audience more quickly. If your content resonates with your target audience, it can lead to faster growth.

Networking and Collaboration: Building relationships and collaborating with others in your industry can expedite your personal brand's growth. Partnerships and endorsements can introduce your brand to wider audiences.

Given these variables, it's challenging to provide a specific timeline you will see results in, and certainly results you can measure. Some individuals might start seeing initial results, such as increased engagement or a growing following, within a few months of consistent effort. However, more substantial results, such as increased business opportunities, career advancements, or significant brand recognition, often take several years of dedicated work. Don't let that make you part of the majority who simply throw up your hands and decide to not measure at all. Neither should you let yourself be seduced into measuring something superficial like your number of followers, when they may never engage or convert into clients or part of your community.

It's essential to remain patient and persistent in your personal branding efforts. Continue to refine your strategy based on data and feedback, and don't be discouraged if you don't see immediate results. Personal branding is a long-term investment, and the rewards tend to accumulate over time as your brand becomes more established and trusted within your industry or niche.

Where To Begin

To measure the success of your brand, it is important to begin with the end in mind. What is your goal? A board position? Ten substantial new clients annually? Not only must this goal drive your brand efforts, it also will define what you need to measure. Your personal brand metrics play a pivotal role by providing tangible benchmarks for measuring your progress, offering clarity in the midst of your branding efforts. With specific goals in mind and key performance indicators (KPIs) in place, metrics give you a clear picture of how your strategies translate into real-world results.

These metrics aren't just numbers; they're tools for identifying the strengths and weaknesses of your personal brand. By analyzing the data they provide, you can refine your strategies, focusing on what truly works. Metrics help ensure that your branding efforts remain aligned with your overarching objectives, acting as a beacon guiding your path.

Moreover, metrics instill a sense of accountability. They encourage consistency and discipline in your branding endeavors, helping you stay the course towards your long-term goals instead of being swayed by short-term fluctuations. As you gather data over time, you gain the power to adapt and optimize your personal brand strategy. If certain tactics aren't yielding the desired results, metrics empower you to pivot and explore new approaches that resonate more effectively with your audience.

Consider various metrics in your personal brand growth journey. From tracking social media engagement and website traffic to evaluating the performance of email marketing campaigns and the effectiveness of your content, these metrics serve as invaluable compasses for guiding your personal brand to success. Networking outcomes, lead generation, audience feedback, and the visibility of your personal brand across platforms are also critical areas to measure. By systematically tracking these metrics, you not only chart the growth of your personal brand but also ensure that it leads you toward your desired career or business outcomes.

Putting Your Metrics Into Practice

While all this metrics stuff might sound great in principle, you may be left wondering what it looks like in actual practice. Here are several examples to help you identify what might work for your personal brand:

Example 1: Social Media Engagement
- **Identification:** Track the number of likes, shares, comments, and follower growth on platforms relevant to your brand, such as Instagram or LinkedIn.
- **Use:** High engagement metrics indicate that your content resonates with your audience. Use this data to identify the types of content and posting schedules that generate the most interaction. Adjust your content strategy accordingly to maintain or increase engagement.

Example 2: Website Traffic
- **Identification:** Monitor the number of visitors, page views, and bounce rate on your website using tools like Google Analytics or built in tools in platforms such as Wix.
- **Use:** Analyze which content on your website attracts the most traffic and keeps visitors engaged. Use this information to tailor your content creation efforts, optimize underperforming pages, and improve the overall user experience.

Example 3: Email Marketing Performance
- **Identification:** Measure open rates, click-through rates, unsubscribe rates, and subscriber growth for your email campaigns.
- **Use:** High open and click-through rates indicate that your email content is resonating with your audience. Conversely, a high unsubscribe rate may signal issues with your email content or frequency. Use these metrics to refine your email marketing strategy, improve content relevance, and segment your audience for more personalized campaigns.

Example 4: Content Effectiveness

- **Identification:** Analyze the reach, engagement (likes, comments, shares), and conversion rates of your content, whether it's blog posts, videos, podcasts, or social media updates.
- **Use:** Identify which types of content perform best in terms of reaching and engaging your audience. If certain topics or formats consistently outperform others, consider producing more of that content to strengthen your personal brand's impact.

Example 5: Networking Outcomes

- **Identification:** Keep a record of the number of meaningful connections, collaborations, or partnerships established as a result of your personal brand efforts.
- **Use:** Assess the quality of your professional network and partnerships. Evaluate whether these connections align with your personal brand goals and help you progress in your career or business. Use this data to prioritize valuable relationships and seek out new opportunities.

Example 6: Personal Brand Visibility

- **Identification:** Monitor your online presence and mentions across different platforms using tools like Google Alerts or social media monitoring software.
- **Use:** Gauge the visibility and reputation of your personal brand in the digital landscape. Track how often you are mentioned, the sentiment of mentions, and which platforms generate the most visibility. Address any negative mentions or issues to protect and enhance your personal brand's image.

These examples demonstrate how identifying and analyzing metrics can provide valuable insights into the effectiveness of your personal brand efforts. By using these metrics strategically, you can refine your branding strategies, make data-driven decisions, and continuously improve your personal brand's impact on your career or business.

Using Metrics to Adapt and Evolve Your Brand

Using metrics to adapt and evolve your personal brand is a dynamic process that allows you to refine your strategies, improve your brand's effectiveness, and stay relevant in your chosen field or industry. When you use them effectively, they provide valuable insights into what's working and what needs adjustment, enabling you to make informed decisions that can have a significant impact on your brand's growth.

One key aspect of using metrics correctly is setting clear objectives and those KPIs we mentioned earlier, from the outset. Thus the KPIs you select become a roadmap for your personal brand growth and guide the metrics you need to track. For example, if your goal is to increase your online presence, you might focus on metrics related to social media engagement, website traffic, or online mentions. By aligning your metrics with your objectives, you ensure that you're measuring what truly matters to your brand's success.

Once you've collected relevant data through your chosen metrics, it's time to analyze the results. Look for patterns and trends within the data to gain a deeper understanding of how your personal brand is performing. Are there specific types of content that consistently generate higher engagement? Do certain times of the day or days of the week yield better results? Are there particular platforms where your audience is more active? Interestingly, I found that while my social media engagement was nominal, I was receiving incoming leads based on my social media content. By asking these leads where they heard of me, and what inspired them to reach out, I found the success metric I never would have originally considered if I had listened to all the pundits telling me to lure them with cold social outreach and buy ads. By answering these questions, you can identify strengths and weaknesses in your personal branding strategy.

With insights in hand, you can begin making data-driven adjustments to your personal brand. For example, if you find that your LinkedIn posts receive more engagement on weekdays, you might shift your posting schedule accordingly. If a particular content format, such as video, garners more attention, you can prioritize creating more video content. Similarly, if you notice that specific topics resonate strongly with your audience, you can focus on producing more content related to those subjects.

Moreover, metrics can help you refine your targeting efforts. By understanding the demographics and preferences of your audience, you can tailor your content and messaging to better meet their needs and interests. This personalization enhances the connection between your brand and your audience, fostering deeper engagement and loyalty.

Effective use of metrics is really non-negotiable for you to adapt and evolve your personal brand strategically. By aligning metrics with your goals, analyzing the data, and making informed adjustments, you can continuously enhance your brand's impact, resonate more effectively with your audience, and achieve your career or business objectives. It's an ongoing process of refinement and optimization that keeps your personal brand dynamic and relevant, whether that is digitally-based, or not.

CHAPTER 10

Your Brand is Your Reputation

The saying goes that *any press is good press*. For some that might be true, but there are a number of cases where that is highly questionable. The "press" now can include fake magazines, online summits hosted by individuals with little or no credibility themselves. It can be "pay to play" features on you or your business that cost anywhere from $250 to $5,000, and many other opportunities with no actual credibility. It's even worse than flushing that cash. Depending on which of these you choose to explore, you can damage your brand faster than you can even imagine, and far, far faster than the time it took to build it.

It is vital you carefully select where to grow your brand's visibility, and ensure you are cultivating not only awareness, but also respect, instead of claiming any visibility opportunity that comes your way at the expense of your hard-earned brand reputation.

Your reputation management is integral to personal branding because it underpins trust, consistency, and credibility in your interactions with others. By upholding your values and delivering on your promises in every outlet you participate in, you not only build a reputable personal brand but also create a strong foundation for lasting success. After all, your brand reputation is the perception others have of you, and it significantly influences how you are perceived in your personal and professional life.

Brands build trust. Yours is no different. That is its first and main function. Trust is the cornerstone of any successful personal brand. When people trust you, they are more likely to engage with your content, do business with you, or support your career advancement. A positive reputation instills confidence for your audience, making them feel comfortable interacting with and endorsing your brand.

The most effective reputation management is closely tied to consistency. A strong personal brand is built on a consistent and authentic image. When your actions align with the values and promises you convey, it reinforces your credibility and builds a reputation for reliability. Consistency helps you create a brand identity that is easily recognizable and memorable to your audience. Now, this may be of little comfort if you are trying to grow your brand rapidly, because it means what it implies: you generate a strong brand reputation over time, not in just days or weeks. We live in an age of fake news. You neither want nor need to contribute to that by racing to exude what you haven't yet earned.

As much effort and time as it can take, maintaining a good reputation serves as a protective shield against negative circumstances or criticism. In the digital age, information spreads rapidly, and one misstep can tarnish your brand's image. By proactively managing your reputation, you can address issues promptly, mitigate damage, and prevent minor setbacks from escalating into major crises.

There simply is no replacement for a positive reputation, which often leads to organic growth and opportunities. When others perceive you as trustworthy and knowledgeable in your field, they are more likely to refer you to new connections, recommend your services, or collaborate with you on projects. Your reputation can open doors to partnerships, speaking engagements, job offers, and more. Unfortunately, this is not only the most important part of building a credible brand, it is the least discussed.

A Good Defense

Protecting your budding personal brand from reputation risks requires vigilance, proactive strategies, and a commitment to maintaining a positive image. Now, keep in mind, a positive image isn't the same thing as ensuring you never offend anyone, and every likes you. Think of "positive" as being an affirmation of your brand values, your mission and vision, your talking points and stance, as well as advocating for your ideal audience. For example, someone who is advocating for women who are harassed or underpaid in the workplace may easily offend an executive who feels their position or status quo is threatened. That does not mean that the women's advocate is not maintaining a positive image.

Regardless, one of the first places most personal brand builders will need to maintain their attention is monitoring your online presence regularly. Set up alerts or use reputation monitoring tools to keep track of mentions, comments, and reviews related to your personal brand. By staying informed, you can promptly address any negative or misleading information that may harm your reputation.

Additionally, be mindful of your online behavior and content. Ensure that your social media posts, comments, and interactions align with your brand's values and message. Avoid engaging in controversial or offensive discussions that could negatively impact your reputation. Remember that the internet has a long memory, and even deleted content can resurface.

Engaging with your audience authentically is another critical aspect of reputation protection. Respond to comments and messages professionally and courteously, even when facing criticism. Address concerns openly and transparently, and take steps to resolve issues promptly. Demonstrating your commitment to customer or audience satisfaction can mitigate the impact of negative feedback.

Moreover, proactively build a network of brand advocates and supporters. Cultivate positive relationships with colleagues, clients, and followers who can vouch for your credibility and professionalism. Positive word-of-mouth and testimonials from satisfied clients or partners can serve as powerful shields against reputation risks.

Lastly, have a crisis management plan in place. Anticipate potential reputation threats and outline the steps to take in case of an issue. Designate a spokesperson if necessary and be prepared to communicate transparently and effectively during challenging times. By planning ahead, you can minimize the damage and maintain trust even when facing adversity. In essence, protecting your personal brand from reputation risks requires ongoing diligence and a commitment to upholding the values and integrity that define your brand.

Managing Your Brand Offline

Of course, protecting your personal brand offline is equally, if not even more important. It involves minimizing reputation risks in real-world interactions. Before you scoff at the implication that this goes without saying, it is actually where I see an unlikely number of personal brand struggle.

Maintaining professionalism and ethical conduct in every offline encounter is not as easy as it might sound. Although you might vigorously agree that consistently upholding integrity, reliability, and respect is essential to your brand, integrity can be one of the first underpinnings of your brand to suffer if you are not actively putting your brand and your integrity first in every interaction.

For example, if you are intent on building a personal brand for your business, you might realize how tempting it could be to blur the line on integrity by making exaggerated claims or misrepresenting your actual capabilities (just a little bit!) to close a deal or gain a competitive advantage. This can involve making promises that you discover you cannot realistically fulfill, overstating your qualifications or experience, or presenting your products or services in a misleadingly positive light. And your brand takes a hit.

We all have likely seen someone trying to secure a lucrative contract who exaggerated their company's track record or inflate the potential benefits of their services to win over a client. While it might seem tempting in the short term, such actions can damage their reputation and erode trust when clients discover the misrepresentation or experience underwhelming results.

Similarly, in the realm of marketing, some businesses might employ deceptive tactics to make their products or services appear superior or more in demand than they actually are. This could include posting fake reviews, manipulating social media metrics, or using misleading advertising practices. Such actions can lead to reputational harm and legal consequences should consumers or competitors uncover the deception.

In the long run, blurring the line on integrity to close deals or misrepresent capabilities can have serious consequences for a personal brand and the associated business. It erodes trust, damages relationships, and can result in legal and ethical ramifications. Proceed at your own risk.

Time management is the second most common corroding factor on personal brand reputation. Alex, is a prime example of this. He was a junior marketing professional, aiming to climb the corporate ladder. To bolster his personal brand, Alex took on numerous projects and roles within his company, eager to demonstrate his dedication and capabilities. However, he quickly spread himself too thin, leading to an inability to complete tasks promptly and respond to internal clients and teammates effectively.

Initially, Alex's willingness to take on various projects earned him a reputation as a highly motivated and ambitious team player. He was tagged as a "high potential" leader. However, as the workload on his plate continued to grow, cracks began to show. Deadlines were missed, and the quality of their work suffered due to the rushed nature of his efforts. This unsurprisingly caused frustration among internal clients who were relying on Alex's contributions, damaging their relationships and undermining the trust Alex's can-do attitude built in the beginning.

Moreover, Alex's inability to respond promptly to team members' queries or provide the necessary support started to hinder collaborative efforts. It got ugly. And fingers were pointed at Alex. The reputation that Alex had built as a reliable and responsive team player began to erode rapidly.

In the long run, this setback in personal brand reputation had a significant impact on Alex's career advancement goals. While he had initially built a positive image as a dedicated professional, his unrealistic view of the workload and responsibilities he could truly handle was what stuck with his team and superiors. Alex was now view as someone who couldn't be relied on in a pinch. It didn't matter that the company did nothing to train him in what was manageable, or saw the situation, and failed to step in and help. Alex became the scapegoat for all of it, and his brand became the casualty.

To recover from this setback, Alex needed to take steps to rebuild his personal brand that required even more work to restore than his initial efforts. This involved reevaluating their commitments, overcommunicating with his superiors about what was expected and how to orient priorities so they were achievable, as well as setting more realistic deadlines and role distribution. Reestablishing trust meant Alex had to take a step back from trying to be the hero, and instead be an effective member of the team.

Like Alex, when you are taking on too much, it can lead to a reputation setback if it compromises one's ability to deliver quality work and maintain responsiveness. Managing one's personal brand involves not only finding and engaging with opportunities but also ensuring that they can be executed effectively and sustainably.

The Company You Keep

A personal brand's reputation is intricately tied to the company an individual keeps through networking, alliances, and partnerships. The old saying, "You are the company you keep," holds true in the world of personal branding. When individuals associate themselves with reputable, credible, and ethical individuals or organizations, it enhances their personal brand's reputation.

Positive networking can be a powerful tool for personal brand enhancement. Associating with accomplished and respected professionals can elevate one's credibility and open doors to new opportunities. Building a network of mentors, industry leaders, and supportive peers not only fosters personal growth but also reflects positively on one's brand. Recommendations and endorsements from these connections can enhance trust and authenticity.

However, it's crucial to consider the potential impact of alliances and partnerships on personal brand reputation. Collaborating with partners who are less professional, less powerful as a brand, or focused on a different audience can undermine your brand's reputation if the alignment is not well-matched. For instance, if your brand is associated with partners who consistently deliver subpar work or lack professionalism, it can cast doubt on your own standards and judgment. Similarly, aligning with partners whose values or audience diverge significantly from your own may confuse your target audience and dilute your brand's focus.

In essence, the company you keep in your networking, alliances, and partnerships plays a pivotal role in shaping your personal brand's reputation. Choosing to associate with respected, ethical, and accomplished individuals or organizations can enhance your brand's credibility, while aligning with partners who may not meet professional standards, have less brand power, or cater to a different audience can pose risks to your reputation. Careful consideration and due diligence in forming these connections are crucial for successful personal brand management.

In brief, it is absolutely okay to be the least accomplished, least brilliant person in the room if those with more established brands are willing to include you. Not attempting to align with bigger or more far-reaching brands is a sure way to keep your reputation struggling.

That's why building strong relationships and networks within your industry or community is another offline safeguard. A robust network can provide support when your reputation is at stake and vouch for your character and expertise when needed. It is the fastest way to open the doors you might otherwise never have access to. These connections can also offer protection and counteract negative perceptions that may arise from unforeseen situations.

Speak for Yourself

Effective communication skills are crucial for resolving conflicts and misunderstandings that can harm your reputation. Managing your personal brand's reputation demands a vigilant focus on communication, since words rapidly shape perceptions others hold of us. The art of communication extends from the mundane to the profound, and every facet is pivotal in maintaining a positive personal brand. It includes active listening, and ensuring your voice is a presence where it can do the most good. But those are the advanced moves.

At the most fundamental level, proofreading and fact-checking are a foundation of effective communication—one too many would-be personal branders overlook. We're all human, and I've certainly included a typo or two, or three or four, in my communications. But if you know you are your own worst proofreader, then get Grammerly or a similar tool immediately. A single typo or factual error can erode credibility and attention to detail, two qualities that are integral to personal branding. Taking the time to ensure your written and spoken communications are accurate and polished is a comparatively small investment that can pay off fast when it comes to your professional image.

Communication in social media is once again one of the key forms of communication that your reputation rests on. In the age of social media, where our thoughts and opinions can be broadcast to a global audience in an instant, exercising caution is paramount. While it's essential to express your views authentically, grandstanding on controversial issues can be a double-edged sword. While your views may resonate with some, they can easily alienate others, potentially damaging your relationships with peers, bosses, and even cost you your job or your career. Most organizations do at least a cursory check of your social media presence when they are considering hiring you for a position or a project—and those social media posts have a very, very long shadow.

That being said, there certainly are situations where taking a principled stance is not grandstanding, but rather an integral part of your personal brand. If your brand aligns with advocating for social justice, environmental causes, or ethical business practices, speaking out is not only consistent, but expected. Sure. You could alienate some individuals, but no brand can please everyone. That's not a brand, that's a bland. In these cases, authenticity and transparency become your allies, provided you express your views respectfully and constructively.

Furthermore, in interpersonal communications, there are instances where standing your ground is not a choice but a necessity, such as when you face harassment or mistreatment in a professional setting. Your personal brand should encompass self-respect and assertiveness as a baseline. In such situations, it's crucial to communicate your concerns clearly, seek support, and, if necessary, explore legal recourse—not to create a needless drama and conflict, which, in extreme cases, can lead to accusations of slander or defamation, entangling you in legal battles that tarnish your personal brand's reputation—but in order to be a clear voice for your brand, with absolute integrity.

In essence, communication is the lifeblood of your personal brand, and its impact spans the spectrum from the mundane to the profound. It requires meticulous attention to detail, strategic restraint in public discourse, and the wisdom to discern when to make a principled stand or seek justice. A thoughtful and deliberate approach to communication is the linchpin that ensures your personal brand not only endures but thrives in an ever-evolving professional landscape.

When You Are Under Attack

When your personal brand faces a crisis or comes under attack, either underserved, or as a result of a damaging error on your part, a carefully planned crisis management strategy is crucial. This is best built in advance, so you can swing into action in the first opportunity—the best response is one that is both well considered and immediate.

Start by assessing the situation comprehensively, understanding the source and potential impact of the attack. It's imperative to maintain composure and avoid impulsive reactions, as knee-jerk responses can exacerbate the situation. Seeking legal counsel, especially for severe attacks, can provide guidance on potential legal ramifications and defamation concerns.

Next, develop a clear response strategy. Determine whether a public or private response is appropriate and craft it with transparency and authenticity. Public responses should acknowledge the issue, provide facts, and express your commitment to resolving concerns while avoiding defensive language. Leveraging your network of supporters and allies can help counter negative narratives, and their positive testimonials can be influential.

Monitor online discussions and social media closely, responding promptly and constructively. Avoid online confrontations and focus on maintaining a professional demeanor. Be prepared for potential media inquiries by developing key messages and designating a spokesperson if needed. Reflect on the experience afterward to learn from it and refine your personal brand management.

Ultimately, rebuilding trust and reputation may take time. Consistently demonstrate your commitment to your brand's values, integrity, and professionalism in both your actions and communications moving forward. With a well-executed crisis management plan, transparency, and unwavering dedication to your brand's principles, you can navigate the storm and emerge with your reputation intact.

CHAPTER 11

Re: Inventing You

Brands are living, growing experiences, constantly being cultivated, curated, adapted and evolving with each interaction. The dynamic nature of personal branding requires continuous attention and evolution. It goes without saying that if you have been reading the book, you are, at some level, reinventing yourself and your personal brand. You might think of it as "just polishing the edges" or upleveling. But, please know, there are times that is the nature of reinvention.

A critical aspect of managing your personal brand is knowing when it's time to rebrand. And now may be the time. You don't need to throw out everything you are and stand for in order to rebrand. Far from it. Just know that rebranding can happen at any time. It may be necessary when your brand's identity no longer aligns with your goals, values, or target audience, which may be in a couple of years as your market shifts, or a couple of decades, or perhaps even longer. And let's not forget that you are changing and evolving too. Significant life changes, career shifts, or shifts in personal values may all signal the need for a rebrand.

Many clients come to me at a point where they believe they are ready for a rebrand, and many of them are right. However, before we embark on that often very costly journey, the first step is to examine what is and isn't working. Brand adaptation and evolution involve a process of reflection and adjustment. It's about assessing your brand's current position and making strategic changes to ensure alignment with your goals and values. This can include refreshing your visual identity, updating your messaging to reflect your evolving expertise, or even shifting your focus to cater to a new target audience. Or it might mean simply tweaking one or two of those things.

Adapting and evolving your brand might also involve staying current with industry trends and technologies to remain relevant and competitive. And those answers are best found in the metrics we discussed in chapter 9. If you don't have metrics, you will have a devil of a time determining what is and isn't working. And throwing the baby out with the bathwater can, in fact, not only be very costly, it can mean starting your brand all over from square one.

If you embark on this brand-building journey, expect a mix of challenges and opportunities—including the need to alter what you thought was solid platinum and would never need to be changed about your brand. Change can be met with resistance, both from within and externally, as your audience adjusts to the new facets of your brand. There may be a need for re-educating them, or even finding a whole new tribe. However, it also opens doors for growth, expanded reach, and increased resonance with a changing or broader audience. Expect that it may take time for your audience to fully embrace and recognize your evolved brand.

When adapting and evolving your brand, look for key indicators of success, such as increased engagement, positive feedback, and a growing and loyal following. Additionally, monitor your progress against your rebranding goals and objectives. Are you effectively conveying your new brand message? Is your visual identity resonating with your audience?

Consider refreshing and modifying various elements of your brand as it grows. This may include updating your logo, redesigning your website, revising your social media presence, or refining your content strategy. Pay attention to the details, from the tone of your messaging to the colors and visuals that represent your brand. Every interaction should reflect the current state of your brand's identity and values.

In essence, the process of brand adaptation and evolution is an ongoing journey that requires careful consideration, strategic planning, and a willingness to embrace change. It's about keeping your brand relevant, authentic, and resonant with your evolving goals and the ever-changing dynamics of your audience and industry. Brands, like people, should grow and evolve to remain impactful and meaningful over time.

The Right Time To Rebrand Yourself

Rebranding yourself is not something that should be done impulsively. However, that is not to say you should never do so. Your essential self remains relatively constant, but your values, experiences, and career trajectories can evolve over time, necessitating adjustments to your personal brand. It's essential to strike a balance between maintaining consistency and adapting to change.

I strongly recommend that everyone conduct periodic brand self-audits. The frequency of these audits can vary depending on personal circumstances and career trajectories, but a common approach is an annual or bi-annual review. These audits allow individuals to assess whether their personal brand aligns with their current goals, values, and expertise, as well as the market environment. A lot of rebranding happened during Covid, for example.

Signs that it may be time to readdress your personal brand can include significant life events, such as career transitions, changes in personal values (yes, they can absolutely change!), or the development of new skills or expertise. If your current brand no longer accurately represents who you are or the direction you want to take in your personal or professional life, it's a clear indication that rebranding is in order.

Additionally, pay attention to feedback and audience reactions. If you notice that your brand messaging is not resonating with your audience or if engagement levels are declining, it's a sign that your personal brand may need adjustments. Similarly, if you find that you're frequently asked to explain your brand or clarify what you represent, it may indicate that your brand is not effectively communicating your identity.

The decision to rebrand yourself should be intentional, driven by a genuine need for alignment with your evolving self and aspirations. It's a process that requires introspection, strategic planning, and a commitment to authenticity. By conducting regular brand audits and staying attuned to changes in your life and career, you can ensure that your personal brand remains a true reflection of who you are and where you're headed.

An Invitation

Are you ready to take your personal brand to the next level? Crafting and nurturing your personal brand can be a deeply rewarding journey, but it can also be a complex and time-consuming process. While it's entirely possible to embark on this journey independently, it's worth considering the incredible advantages of seeking professional assistance.

Our team of personal branding experts is here to support you every step of the way. Whether you're an entrepreneur looking to grow your business, a professional aiming for career advancement, or simply someone wanting to refine your online presence, our personalized guidance can make a significant difference.

Statistics show that a well-crafted personal brand can have a profound impact on business growth. In fact, studies reveal that businesses with strong personal brands grow 70% faster than those without. This isn't just a number; it's a testament to the real-world advantages that a compelling personal brand can offer.

By working with our team, you'll gain access to invaluable insights, strategies, and techniques that can accelerate your personal branding journey. You'll learn how to avoid common pitfalls and leverage your unique strengths to stand out in a crowded digital landscape.

Remember, personal branding is an investment in yourself, your career, and your business. It's an opportunity to shape how you're perceived by others and create a lasting impact. If you're ready to unlock your full potential and build a personal brand that sets you up for success, we invite you to explore how our professional assistance can make a difference. Let's embark on this transformative journey together.

ABOUT THE AUTHOR

Stacey Ruth is unstoppable, working at the intersection of leadership, intuition, innovation and personal branding. She is the founder and CEO of the Unstoppable Leader. A 30-year veteran entrepreneur, she built two multimillion-dollar agencies, has been among the Top 50 Entrepreneurs Under 50 in Atlanta, and twice awarded Top 100 "It" Agencies by Experiential Marketer. Today she is also a licensed Metaphysical Minister and holds certifications in executive leadership coaching, neuroscience and positive psychology. Her award-winning, best-selling books, *Own Your Own Shift* and *Inside Out Smart* are available on Amazon, Barnes & Noble and other fine retailers